Kate & William

JOHNSTON

◆

COLLINS

◆

ERSKINE

◆

JOLLANDS

◆

SHARMAN

A VERY PUBLIC LOVE STORY

AAM/MARKOSIA

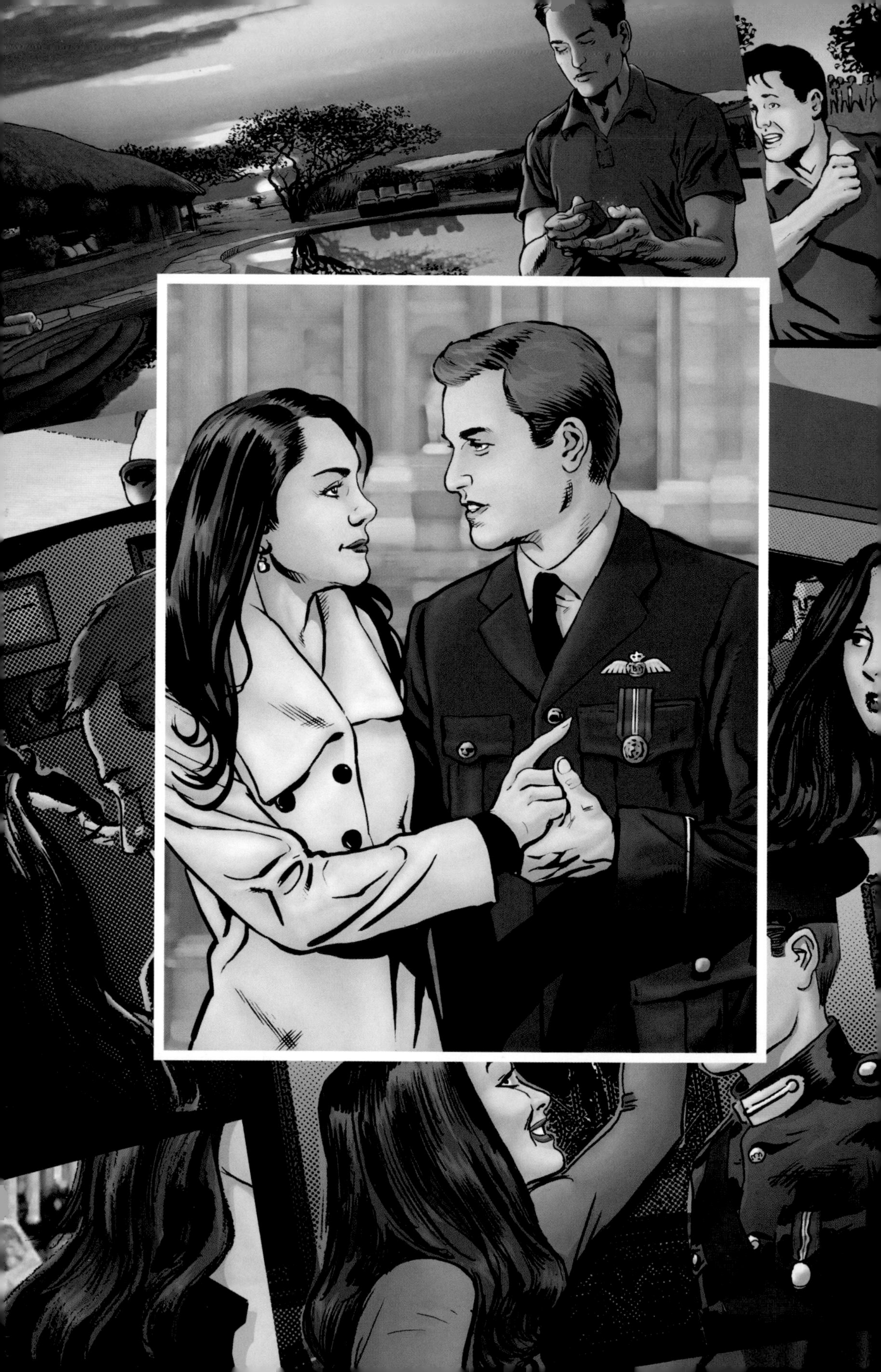

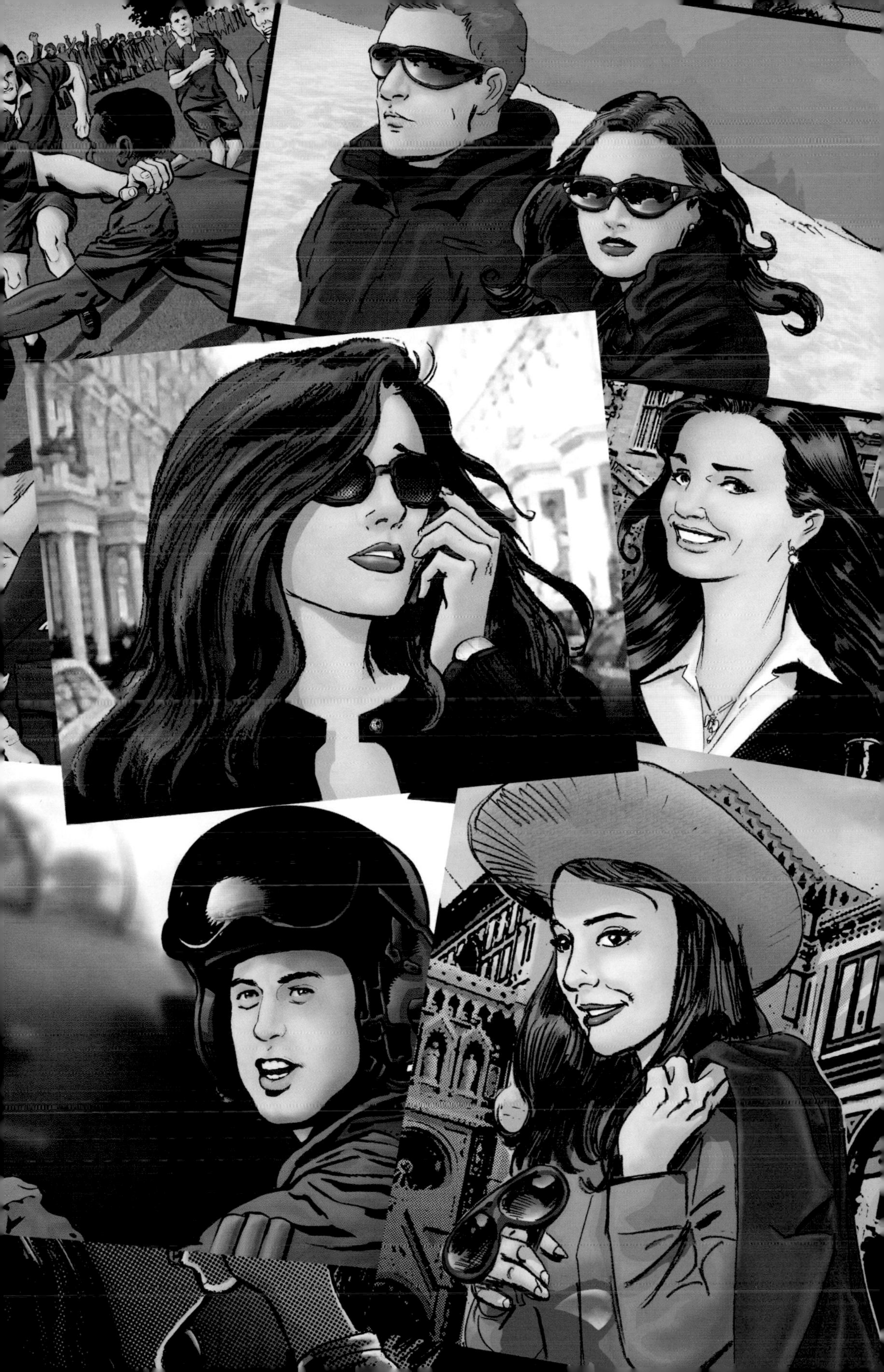

Kate Middleton

A VERY PRIVATE PRINCESS

Written by: **Rich Johnston**

Art by: **Mike Collins**

Colours by: **Owen Jollands of Hayena Studios**

Letters by: **Ian Sharman**

Pin ups: **Paul Green**

THIS IS A FLIP BOOK:
If you'd like to start reading with William's story,
please flip the book over and begin reading
from the other end!

For Markosia Enterprises Ltd

Harry Markos
Publisher & Managing partner

Huw-J
Art Director

Ian Sharman ✦ GM Jordan ✦ Andy Briggs
Group Editors

ISBN: 978-1905692-45-3

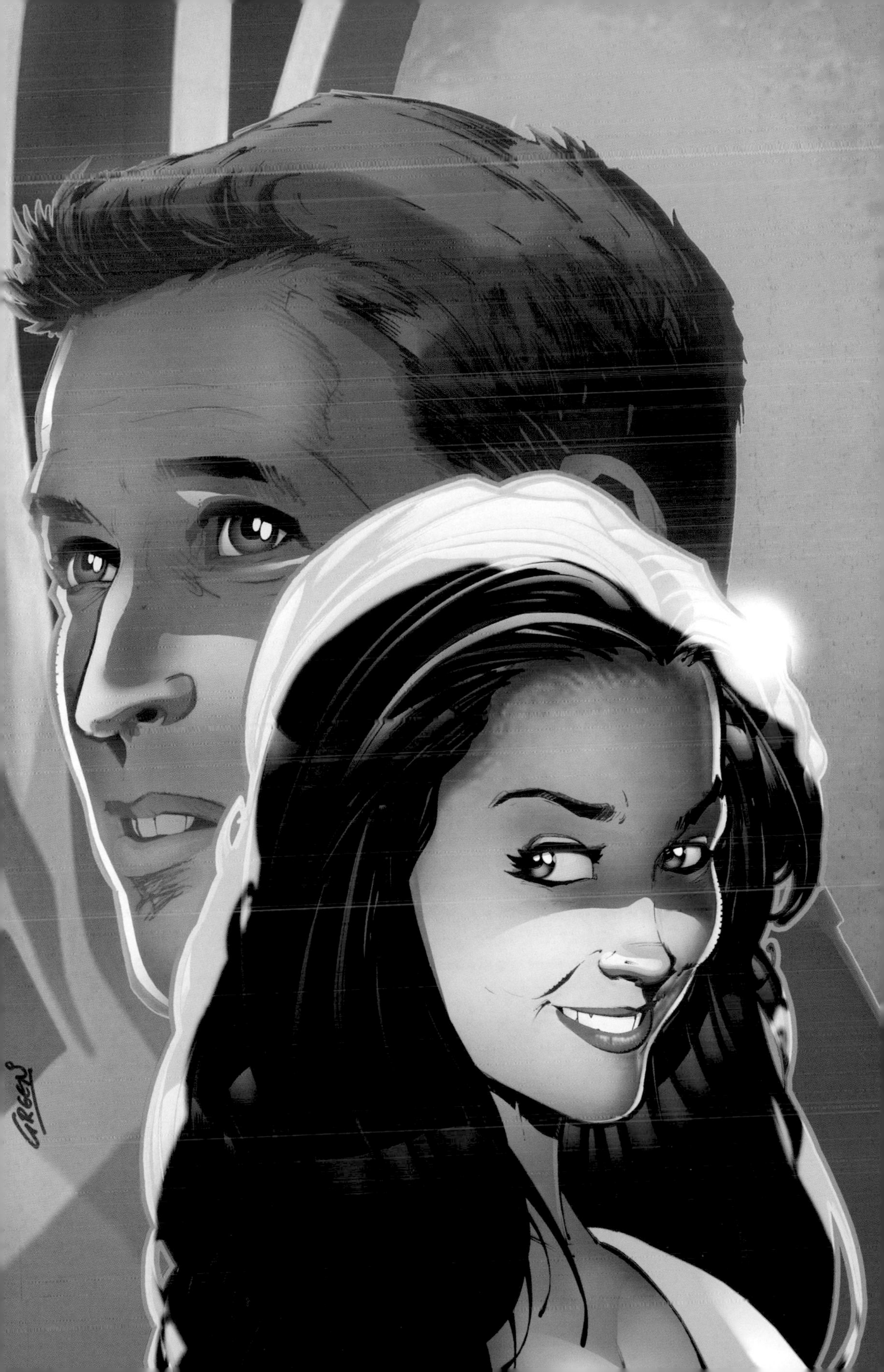
GREEN

Kate Middleton

A Very Private Princess

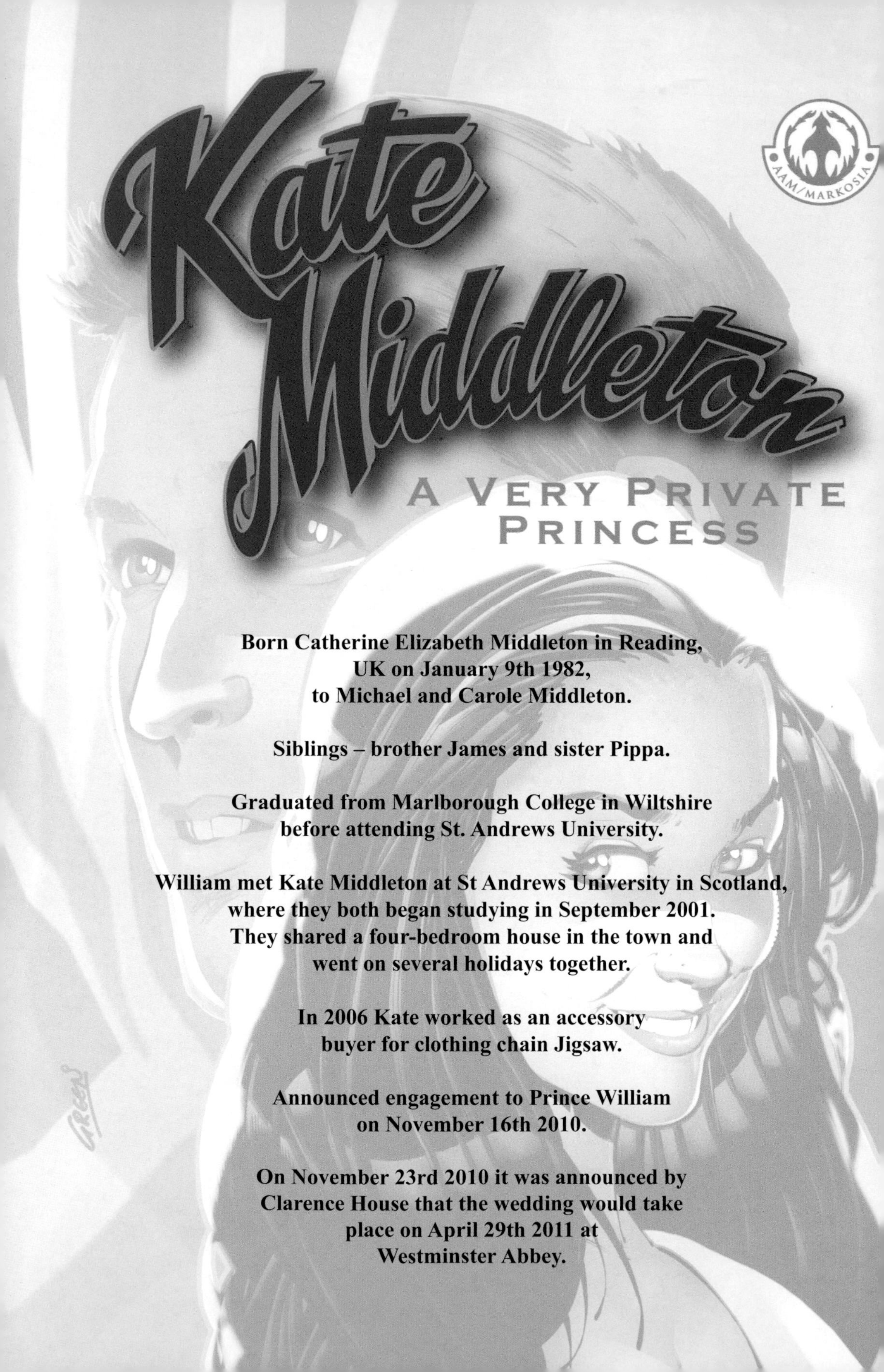

Born Catherine Elizabeth Middleton in Reading, UK on January 9th 1982, to Michael and Carole Middleton.

Siblings – brother James and sister Pippa.

Graduated from Marlborough College in Wiltshire before attending St. Andrews University.

William met Kate Middleton at St Andrews University in Scotland, where they both began studying in September 2001. They shared a four-bedroom house in the town and went on several holidays together.

In 2006 Kate worked as an accessory buyer for clothing chain Jigsaw.

Announced engagement to Prince William on November 16th 2010.

On November 23rd 2010 it was announced by Clarence House that the wedding would take place on April 29th 2011 at Westminster Abbey.

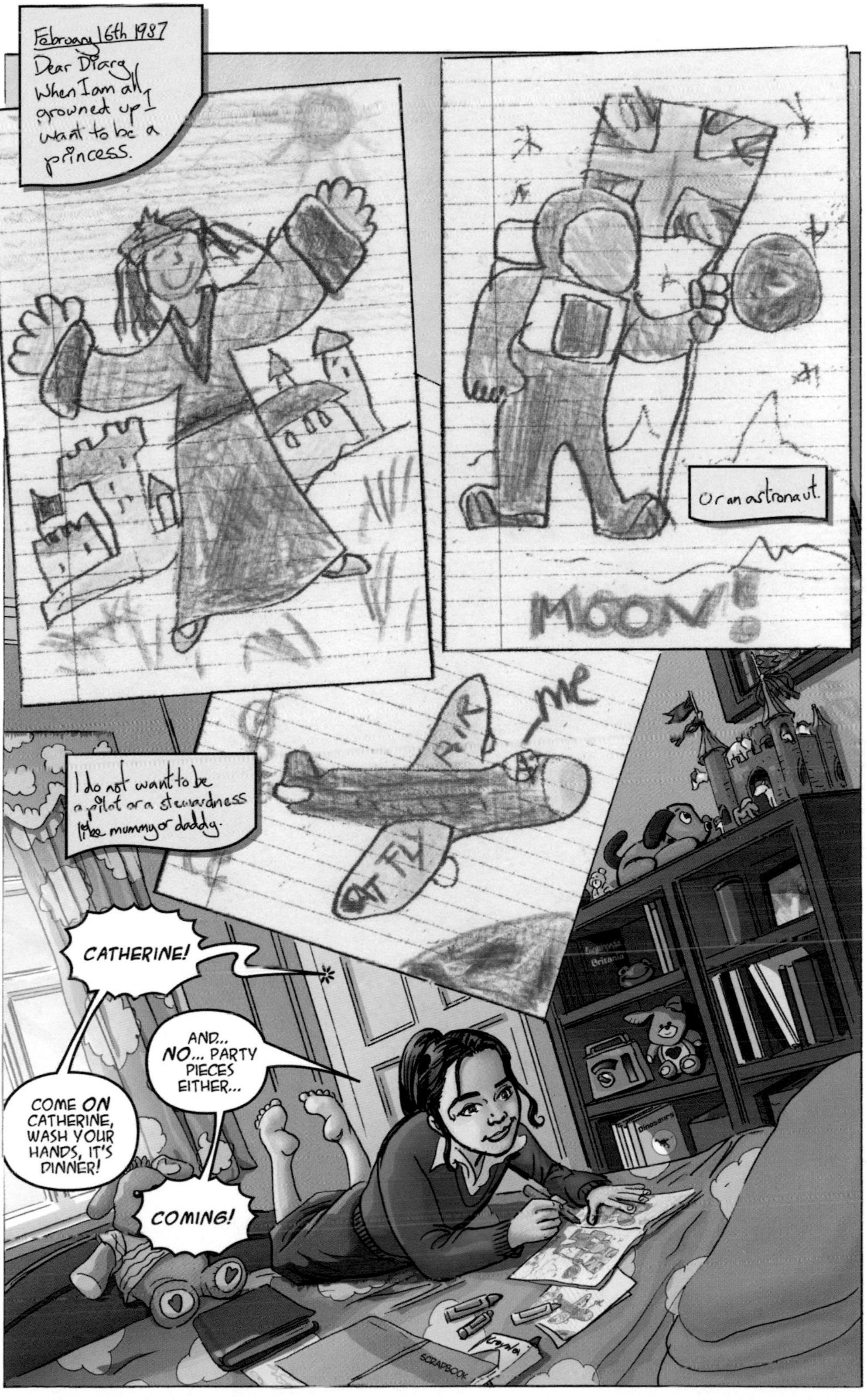
February 16th 1987
Dear Diary
When I am all growned up I want to be a princess.
Or an astronaut.
MOON!
I do not want to be a pilot or a stewardness like mummy or daddy.
AIR
ME
FLY
CATHERINE!
AND... NO... PARTY PIECES EITHER...
COME ON CATHERINE, WASH YOUR HANDS, IT'S DINNER!
COMING!
Dinosaurs
SCRAPBOOK

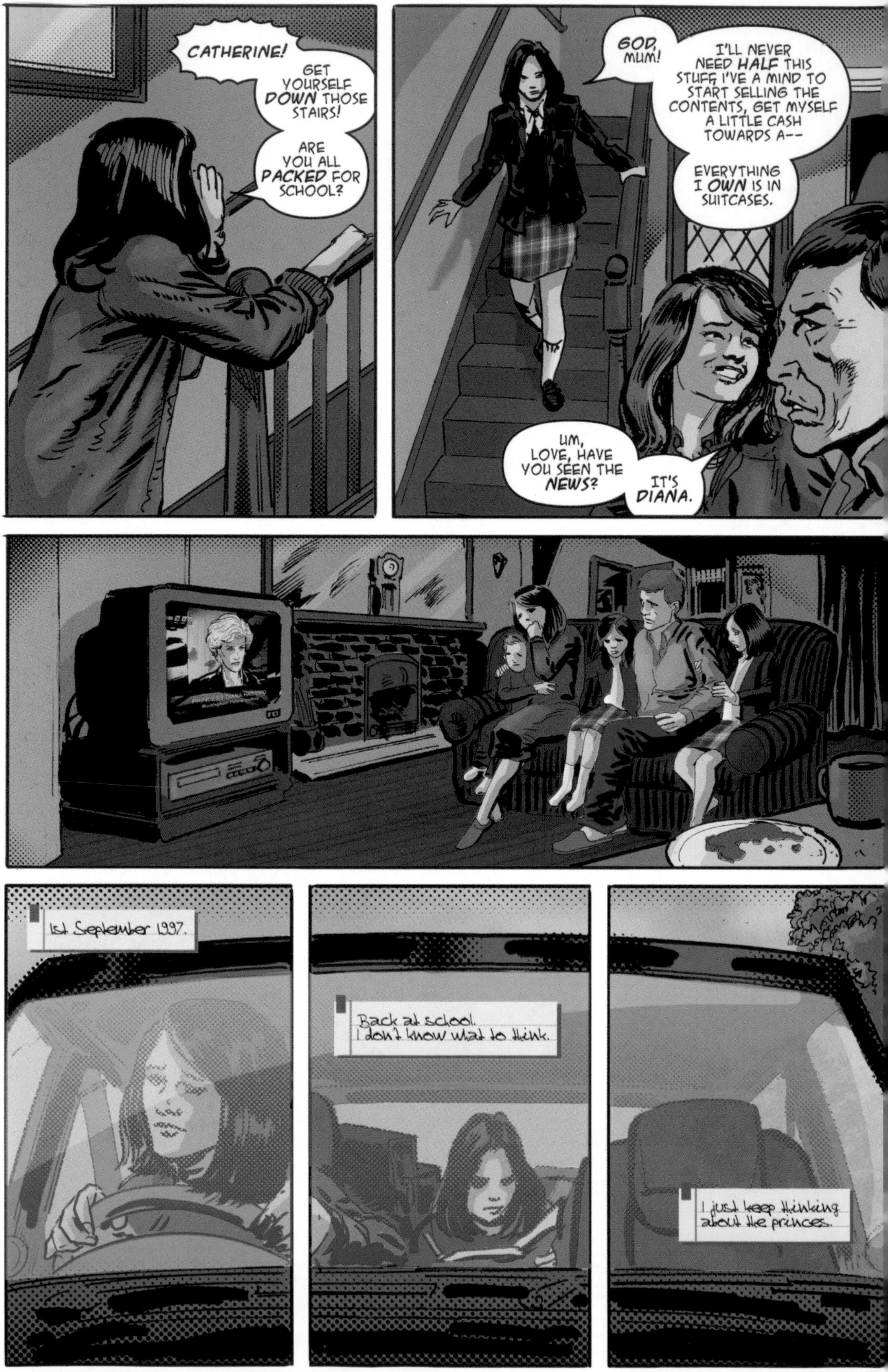
CATHERINE!
GET YOURSELF DOWN THOSE STAIRS!
ARE YOU ALL PACKED FOR SCHOOL?
GOD, MUM!
I'LL NEVER NEED HALF THIS STUFF. I'VE A MIND TO START SELLING THE CONTENTS, GET MYSELF A LITTLE CASH TOWARDS A--
EVERYTHING I OWN IS IN SUITCASES.
UM, LOVE, HAVE YOU SEEN THE NEWS?
IT'S DIANA.
1st September 1997.
Back at school.
I don't know what to think.
I just keep thinking about the princes.

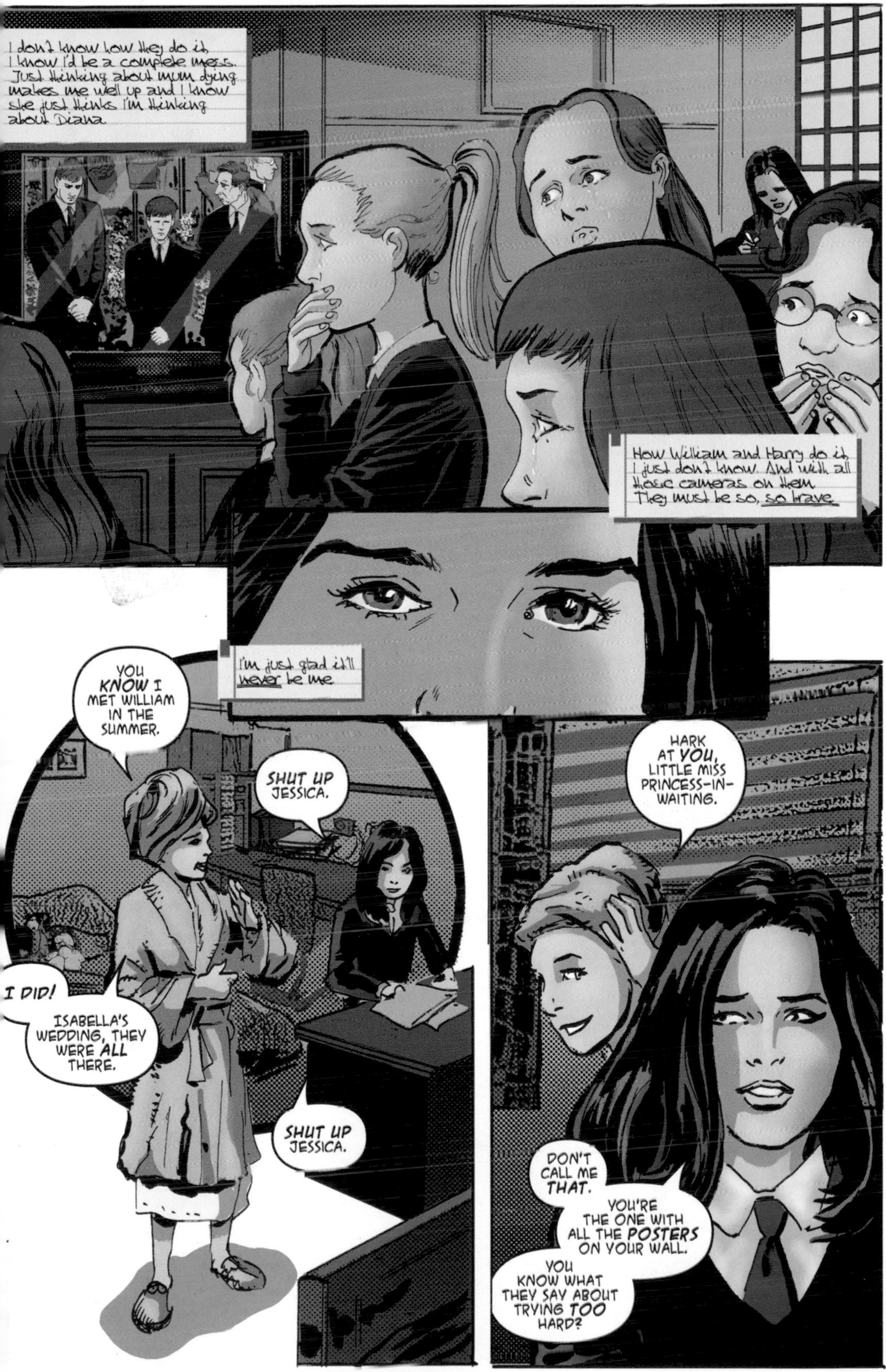
I don't know how they do it. I know I'd be a complete mess. Just thinking about mum dying makes me well up and I know she just thinks I'm thinking about Diana.
How William and Harry do it, I just don't know. And with all those cameras on them. They must be so, so brave.
I'm just glad it'll never be me.
YOU KNOW I MET WILLIAM IN THE SUMMER.
SHUT UP JESSICA.
I DID!
ISABELLA'S WEDDING, THEY WERE ALL THERE.
SHUT UP JESSICA.
HARK AT YOU, LITTLE MISS PRINCESS-IN-WAITING.
DON'T CALL ME THAT.
YOU'RE THE ONE WITH ALL THE POSTERS ON YOUR WALL.
YOU KNOW WHAT THEY SAY ABOUT TRYING TOO HARD?

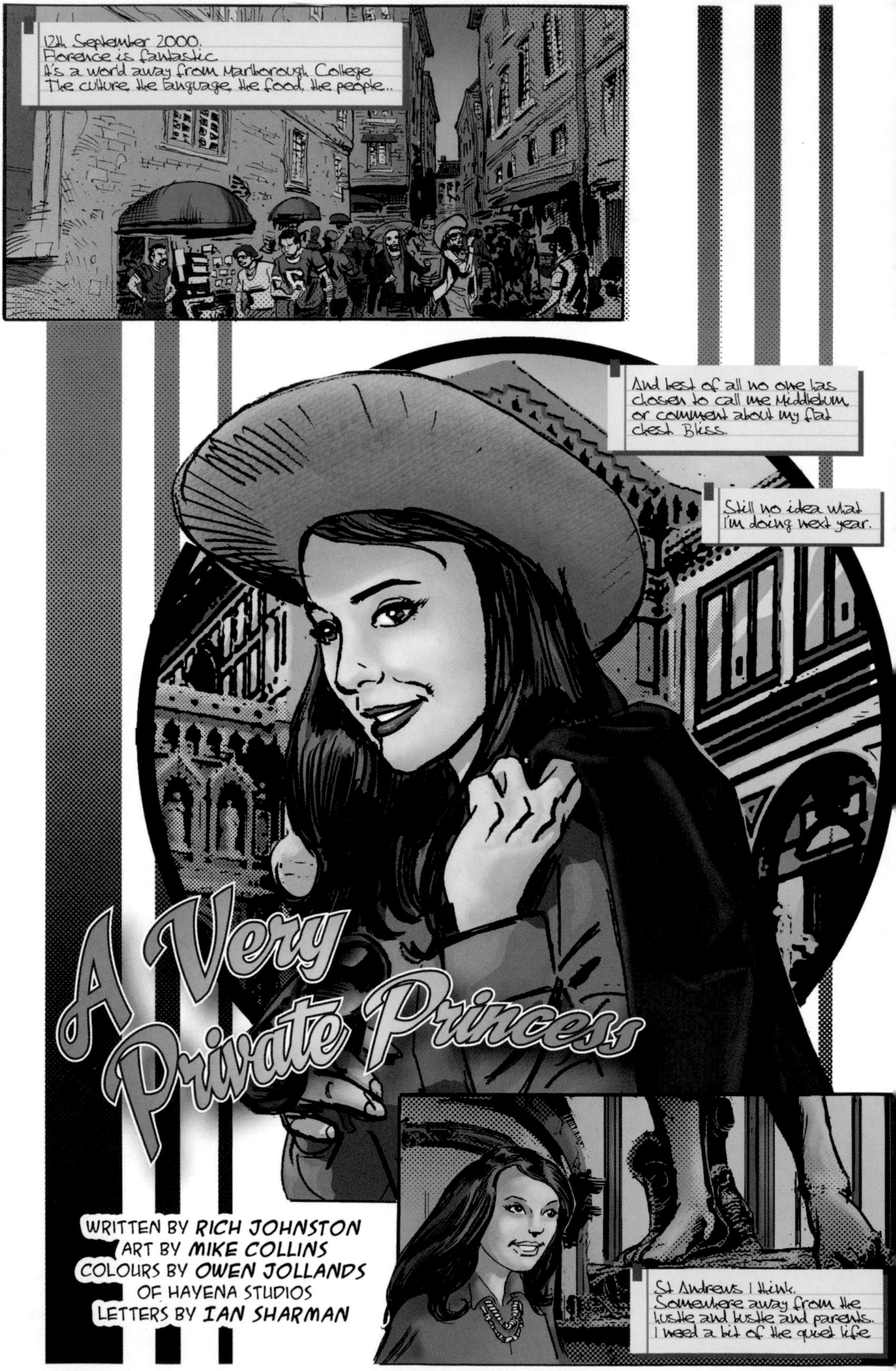
12th September 2000.
Florence is fantastic.
It's a world away from Marlborough College.
The culture, the language, the food, the people...
And best of all no one has chosen to call me Middlebum, or comment about my flat chest. Bliss.
Still no idea what I'm doing next year.
A Very Private Princess
WRITTEN BY RICH JOHNSTON
ART BY MIKE COLLINS
COLOURS BY OWEN JOLLANDS
OF HAYENA STUDIOS
LETTERS BY IAN SHARMAN
St Andrews I think.
Somewhere away from the hustle and bustle and parents.
I need a bit of the quiet life

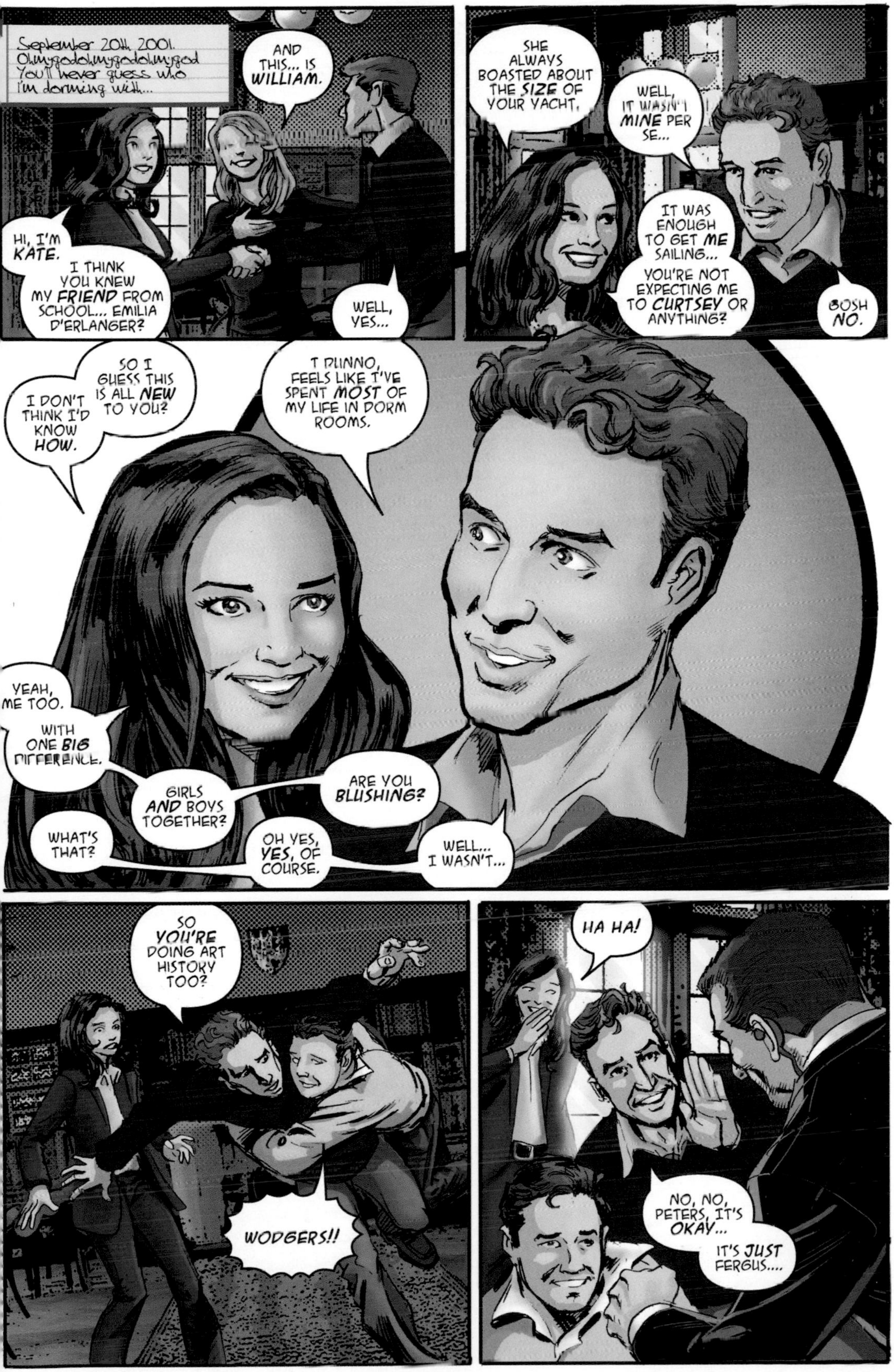

September 20th 2001. Ohmygodohmygodohmygod You'll never guess who I'm dorming with...
AND THIS... IS WILLIAM.
HI, I'M KATE.
I THINK YOU KNEW MY FRIEND FROM SCHOOL... EMILIA D'ERLANGER?
WELL, YES...
SHE ALWAYS BOASTED ABOUT THE SIZE OF YOUR YACHT.
WELL, IT WASN'T MINE PER SE...
IT WAS ENOUGH TO GET ME SAILING...
YOU'RE NOT EXPECTING ME TO CURTSEY OR ANYTHING?
BOSH NO.
SO I GUESS THIS IS ALL NEW TO YOU?
I DON'T THINK I'D KNOW HOW.
I DUNNO, FEELS LIKE I'VE SPENT MOST OF MY LIFE IN DORM ROOMS.
YEAH, ME TOO.
WITH ONE BIG DIFFERENCE.
GIRLS AND BOYS TOGETHER?
WHAT'S THAT?
OH YES, YES, OF COURSE.
ARE YOU BLUSHING?
WELL... I WASN'T...
SO YOU'RE DOING ART HISTORY TOO?
WODGERS!!
HA HA!
NO, NO, PETERS, IT'S OKAY...
IT'S JUST FERGUS....

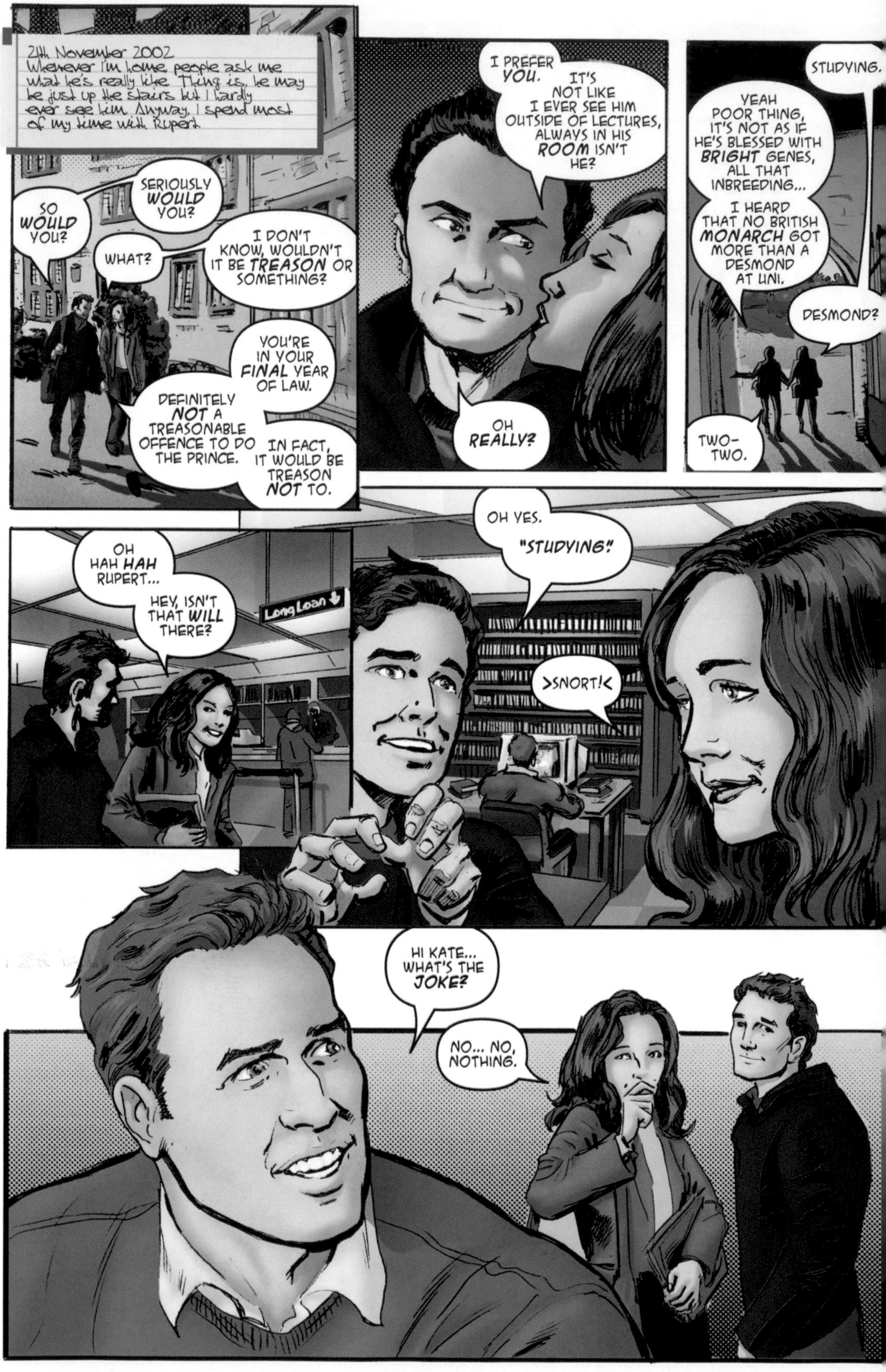
21th November 2002
Whenever I'm home, people ask me what he's really like. Thing is, he may be just up the stairs but I hardly ever see him. Anyway, I spend most of my time with Rupert.
SO WOULD YOU?
SERIOUSLY WOULD YOU?
WHAT?
I DON'T KNOW, WOULDN'T IT BE TREASON OR SOMETHING?
YOU'RE IN YOUR FINAL YEAR OF LAW.
DEFINITELY NOT A TREASONABLE OFFENCE TO DO THE PRINCE.
IN FACT, IT WOULD BE TREASON NOT TO.
I PREFER YOU.
IT'S NOT LIKE I EVER SEE HIM OUTSIDE OF LECTURES, ALWAYS IN HIS ROOM ISN'T HE?
OH REALLY?
STUDYING.
YEAH POOR THING, IT'S NOT AS IF HE'S BLESSED WITH BRIGHT GENES, ALL THAT INBREEDING...
I HEARD THAT NO BRITISH MONARCH GOT MORE THAN A DESMOND AT UNI.
DESMOND?
TWO-TWO.
OH HAH HAH RUPERT...
HEY, ISN'T THAT WILL THERE?
Long Loan
OH YES.
"STUDYING."
>SNORT!<
HI KATE... WHAT'S THE JOKE?
NO... NO, NOTHING.

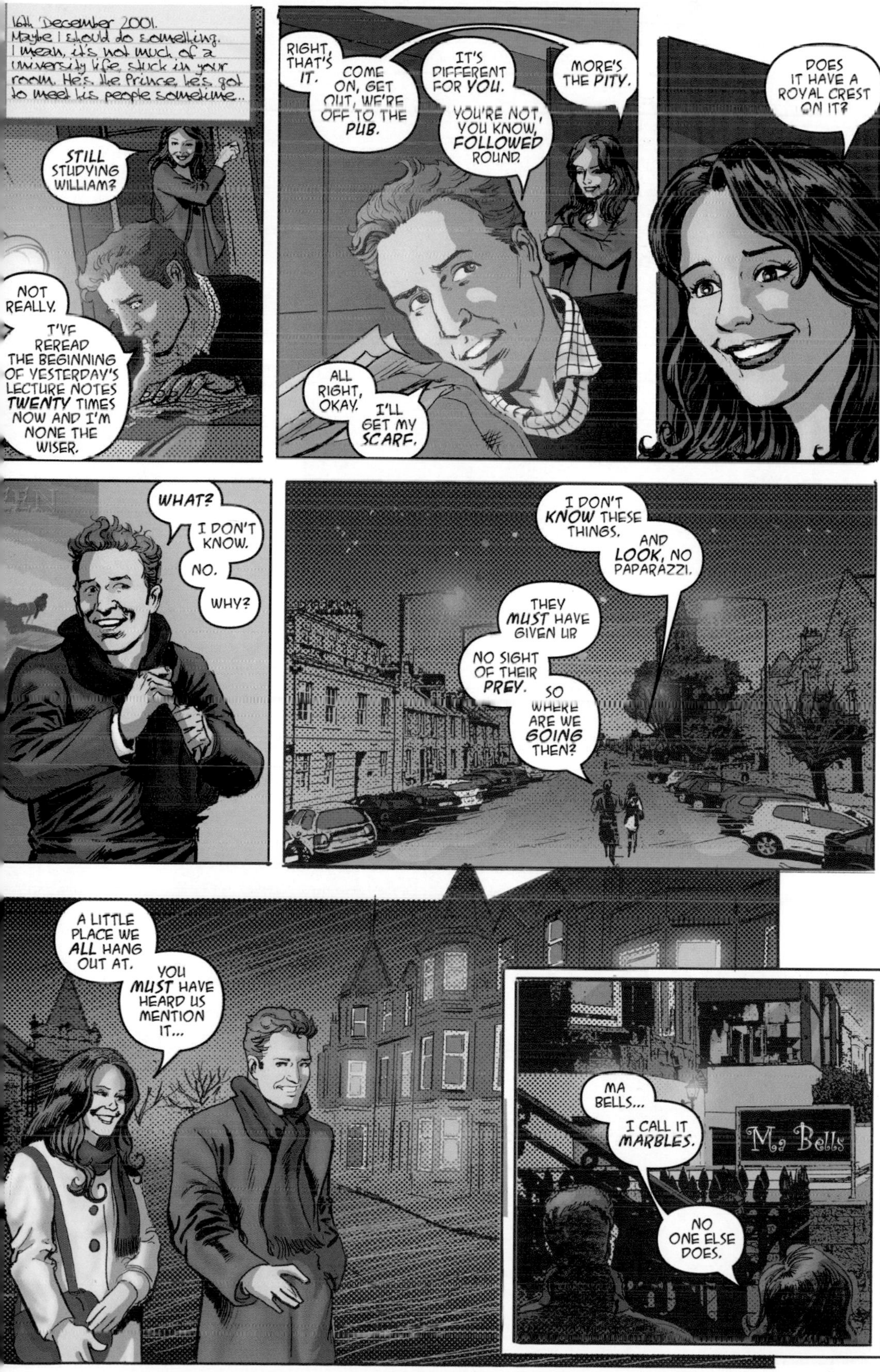

16th December 2001.
Maybe I should do something.
I mean, it's not much of a university life, stuck in your room. He's the Prince, he's got to meet his people sometime...
STILL STUDYING WILLIAM?
NOT REALLY.
I'VE REREAD THE BEGINNING OF YESTERDAY'S LECTURE NOTES TWENTY TIMES NOW AND I'M NONE THE WISER.
RIGHT, THAT'S IT.
COME ON, GET OUT, WE'RE OFF TO THE PUB.
IT'S DIFFERENT FOR YOU.
YOU'RE NOT, YOU KNOW, FOLLOWED ROUND.
MORE'S THE PITY.
ALL RIGHT, OKAY.
I'LL GET MY SCARF.
DOES IT HAVE A ROYAL CREST ON IT?
WHAT?
I DON'T KNOW.
NO.
WHY?
I DON'T KNOW THESE THINGS.
AND LOOK, NO PAPARAZZI.
THEY MUST HAVE GIVEN UP.
NO SIGHT OF THEIR PREY.
SO WHERE ARE WE GOING THEN?
A LITTLE PLACE WE ALL HANG OUT AT.
YOU MUST HAVE HEARD US MENTION IT...
MA BELLS...
I CALL IT MARBLES.
NO ONE ELSE DOES.
Ma Bells

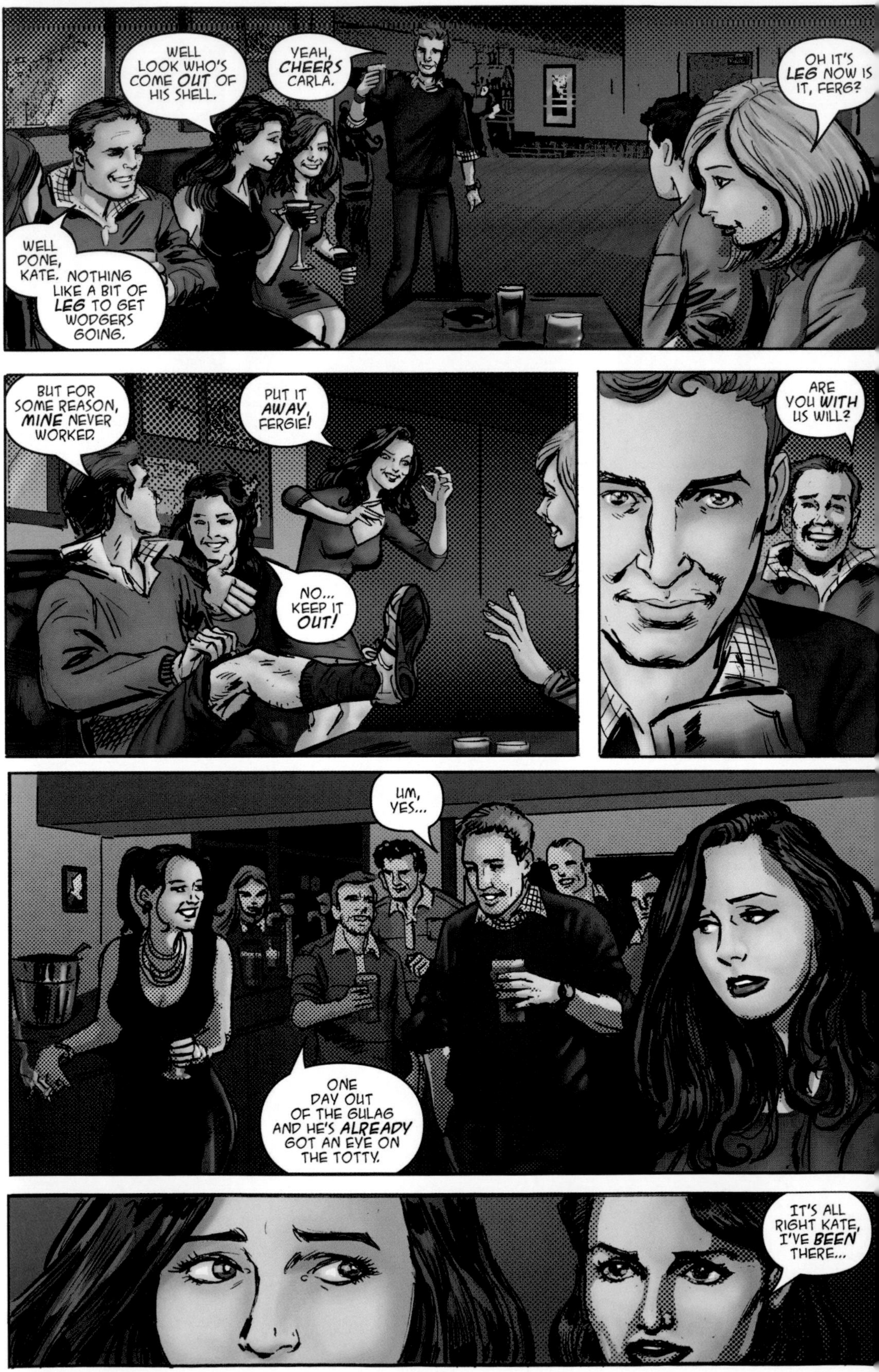

WELL LOOK WHO'S COME OUT OF HIS SHELL.
YEAH, CHEERS CARLA.
OH IT'S LEG NOW IS IT, FERG?
WELL DONE, KATE. NOTHING LIKE A BIT OF LEG TO GET WODGERS GOING.
BUT FOR SOME REASON, MINE NEVER WORKED.
PUT IT AWAY, FERGIE!
NO... KEEP IT OUT!
ARE YOU WITH US WILL?
UM, YES...
ONE DAY OUT OF THE GULAG AND HE'S ALREADY GOT AN EYE ON THE TOTTY.
IT'S ALL RIGHT KATE, I'VE BEEN THERE...

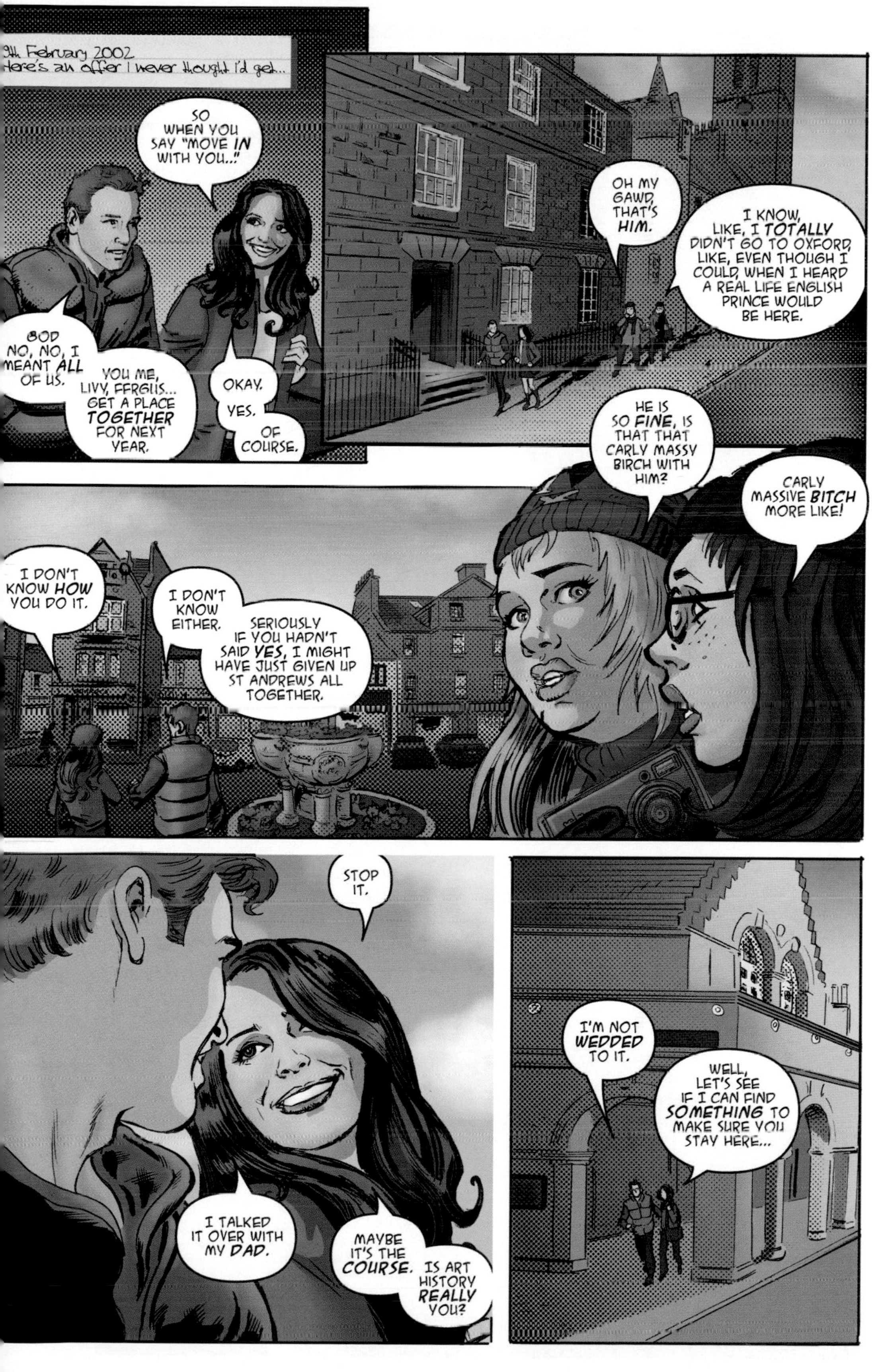
9th February 2002
Here's an offer I never thought I'd get...
SO WHEN YOU SAY "MOVE IN WITH YOU..."
GOD NO, NO, I MEANT ALL OF US.
YOU ME, LIVY, FERGUS... GET A PLACE TOGETHER FOR NEXT YEAR.
OKAY.
YES.
OF COURSE.
OH MY GAWD, THAT'S HIM.
I KNOW, LIKE, I TOTALLY DIDN'T GO TO OXFORD, LIKE, EVEN THOUGH I COULD, WHEN I HEARD A REAL LIFE ENGLISH PRINCE WOULD BE HERE.
HE IS SO FINE, IS THAT THAT CARLY MASSY BIRCH WITH HIM?
CARLY MASSIVE BITCH MORE LIKE!
I DON'T KNOW HOW YOU DO IT.
I DON'T KNOW EITHER.
SERIOUSLY IF YOU HADN'T SAID YES, I MIGHT HAVE JUST GIVEN UP ST ANDREWS ALL TOGETHER.
STOP IT.
I TALKED IT OVER WITH MY DAD.
MAYBE IT'S THE COURSE.
IS ART HISTORY REALLY YOU?
I'M NOT WEDDED TO IT.
WELL, LET'S SEE IF I CAN FIND SOMETHING TO MAKE SURE YOU STAY HERE...

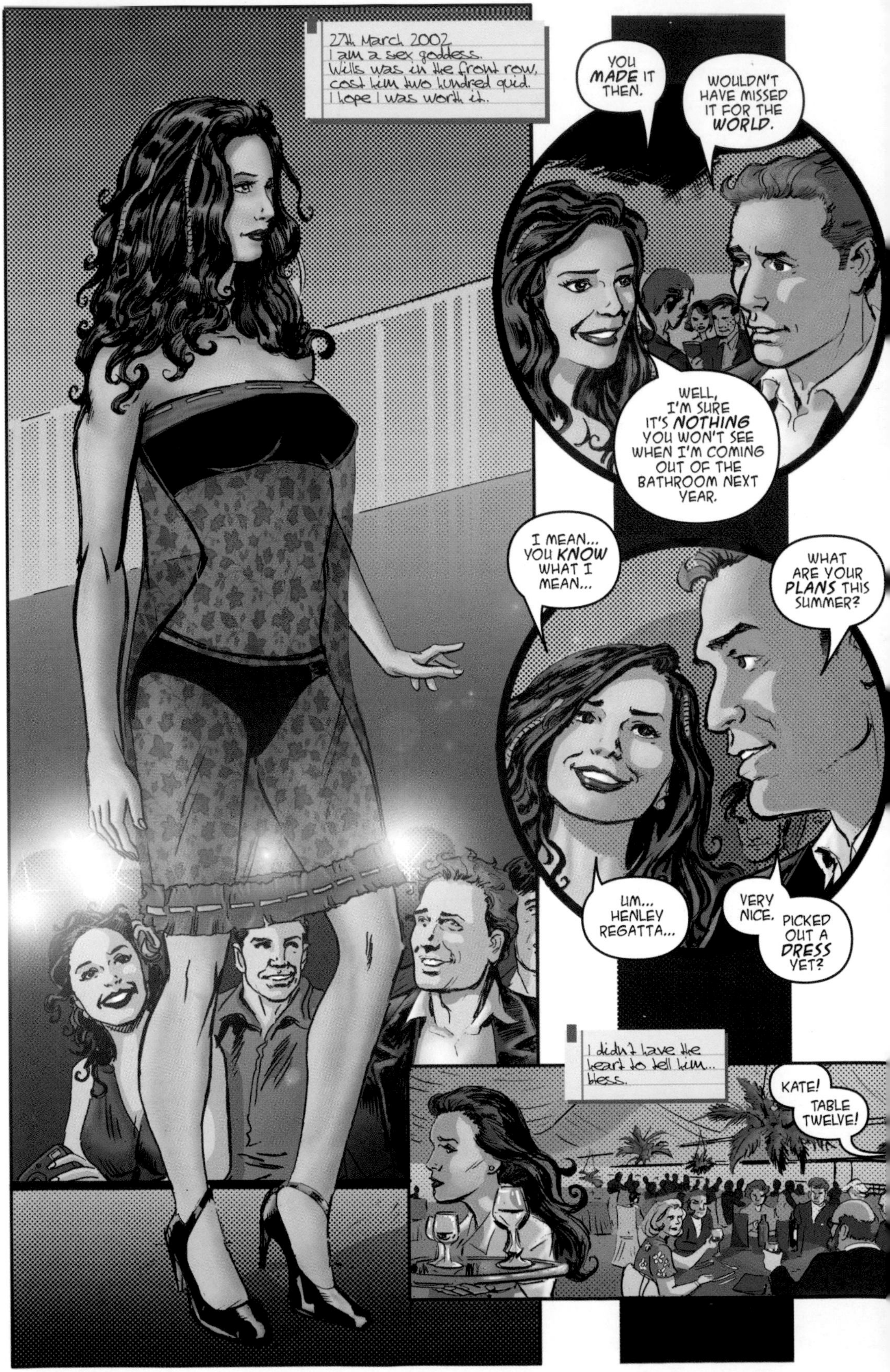

27th March 2002
I am a sex goddess.
Wills was in the front row,
cost him two hundred quid.
I hope I was worth it.
YOU MADE IT THEN.
WOULDN'T HAVE MISSED IT FOR THE WORLD.
WELL, I'M SURE IT'S NOTHING YOU WON'T SEE WHEN I'M COMING OUT OF THE BATHROOM NEXT YEAR.
I MEAN... YOU KNOW WHAT I MEAN...
WHAT ARE YOUR PLANS THIS SUMMER?
UM... HENLEY REGATTA...
VERY NICE.
PICKED OUT A DRESS YET?
I didn't have the heart to tell him... bless.
KATE!
TABLE TWELVE!

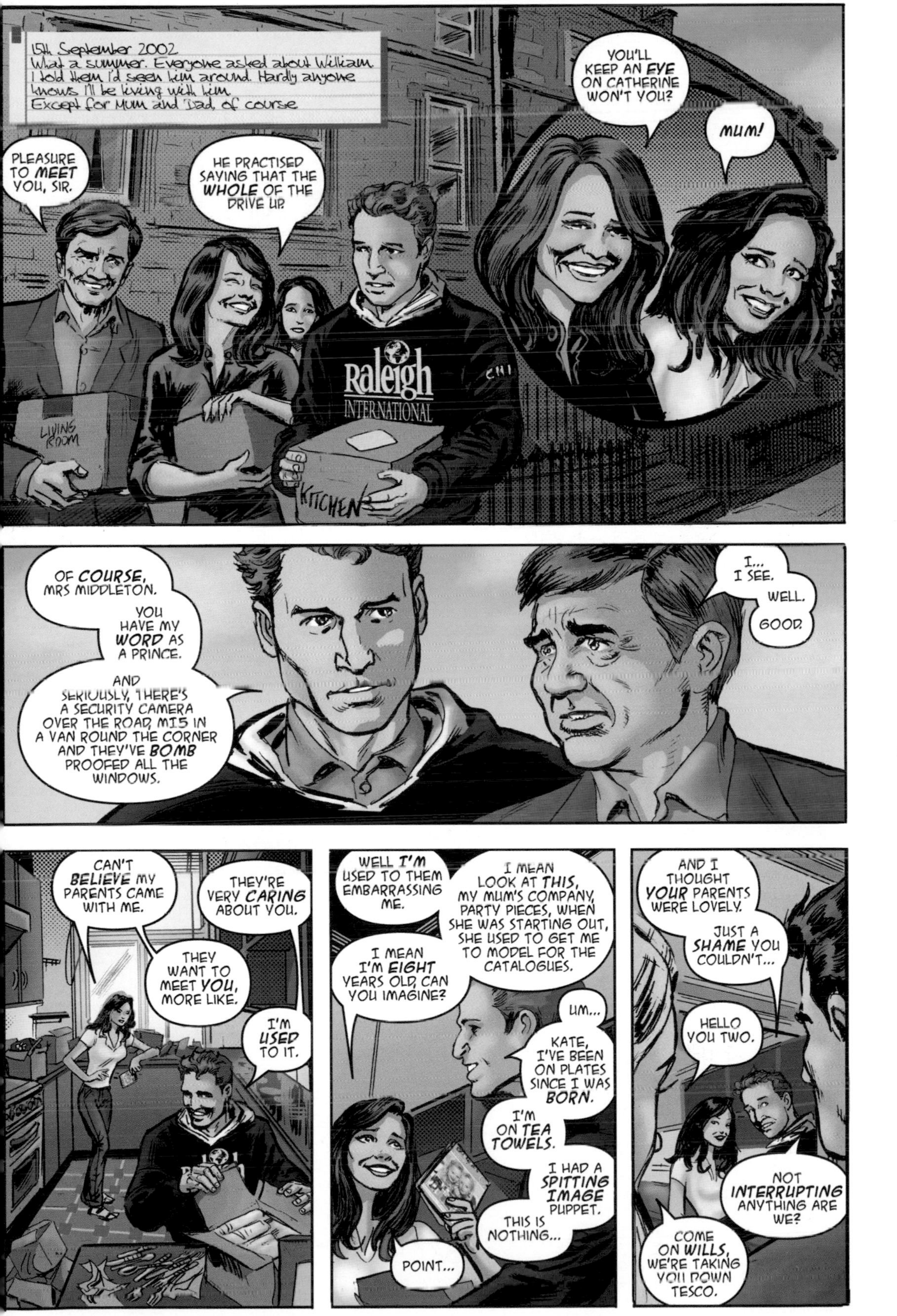
15th September 2002
What a summer. Everyone asked about William.
I told them I'd seen him around. Hardly anyone
knows I'll be living with him.
Except for Mum and Dad, of course
PLEASURE TO MEET YOU, SIR.
HE PRACTISED SAYING THAT THE WHOLE OF THE DRIVE UP.
YOU'LL KEEP AN EYE ON CATHERINE WON'T YOU?
MUM!
Raleigh INTERNATIONAL
LIVING ROOM
KITCHEN
OF COURSE, MRS MIDDLETON.
YOU HAVE MY WORD AS A PRINCE.
AND SERIOUSLY, THERE'S A SECURITY CAMERA OVER THE ROAD, MI5 IN A VAN ROUND THE CORNER AND THEY'VE BOMB PROOFED ALL THE WINDOWS.
I... I SEE.
WELL.
GOOD.
CAN'T BELIEVE MY PARENTS CAME WITH ME.
THEY'RE VERY CARING ABOUT YOU.
THEY WANT TO MEET YOU, MORE LIKE.
I'M USED TO IT.
WELL I'M USED TO THEM EMBARRASSING ME.
I MEAN LOOK AT THIS, MY MUM'S COMPANY, PARTY PIECES, WHEN SHE WAS STARTING OUT, SHE USED TO GET ME TO MODEL FOR THE CATALOGUES.
I MEAN I'M EIGHT YEARS OLD, CAN YOU IMAGINE?
UM...
KATE, I'VE BEEN ON PLATES SINCE I WAS BORN.
I'M ON TEA TOWELS.
I HAD A SPITTING IMAGE PUPPET.
THIS IS NOTHING...
POINT...
AND I THOUGHT YOUR PARENTS WERE LOVELY.
JUST A SHAME YOU COULDN'T...
HELLO YOU TWO.
NOT INTERRUPTING ANYTHING ARE WE?
COME ON WILLS, WE'RE TAKING YOU DOWN TESCO.

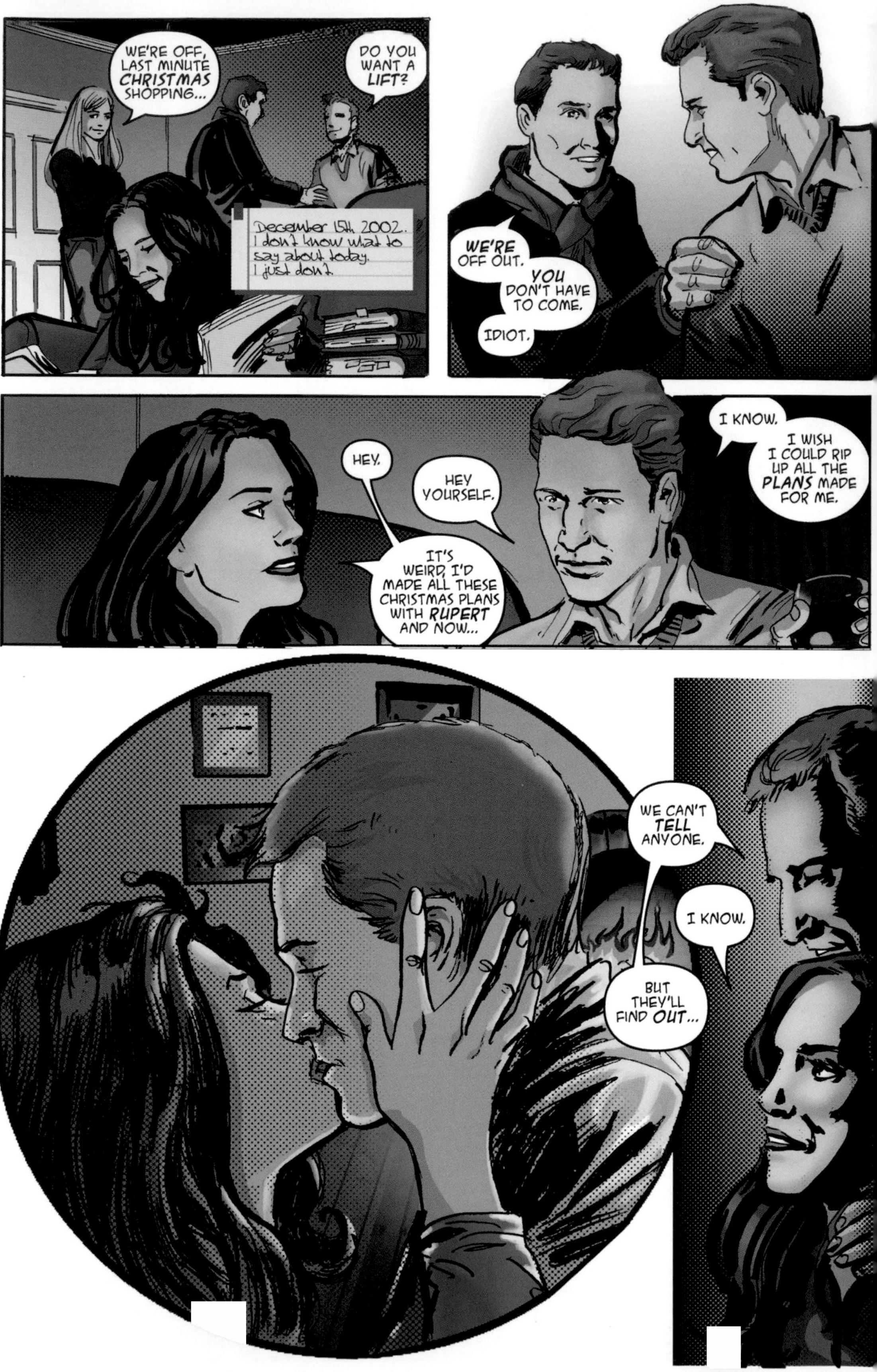
WE'RE OFF, LAST MINUTE CHRISTMAS SHOPPING...
DO YOU WANT A LIFT?
December 15th 2002. I don't know what to say about today. I just don't.
WE'RE OFF OUT.
YOU DON'T HAVE TO COME.
IDIOT.
HEY.
HEY YOURSELF.
IT'S WEIRD, I'D MADE ALL THESE CHRISTMAS PLANS WITH RUPERT AND NOW...
I KNOW.
I WISH I COULD RIP UP ALL THE PLANS MADE FOR ME.
WE CAN'T TELL ANYONE.
I KNOW.
BUT THEY'LL FIND OUT...

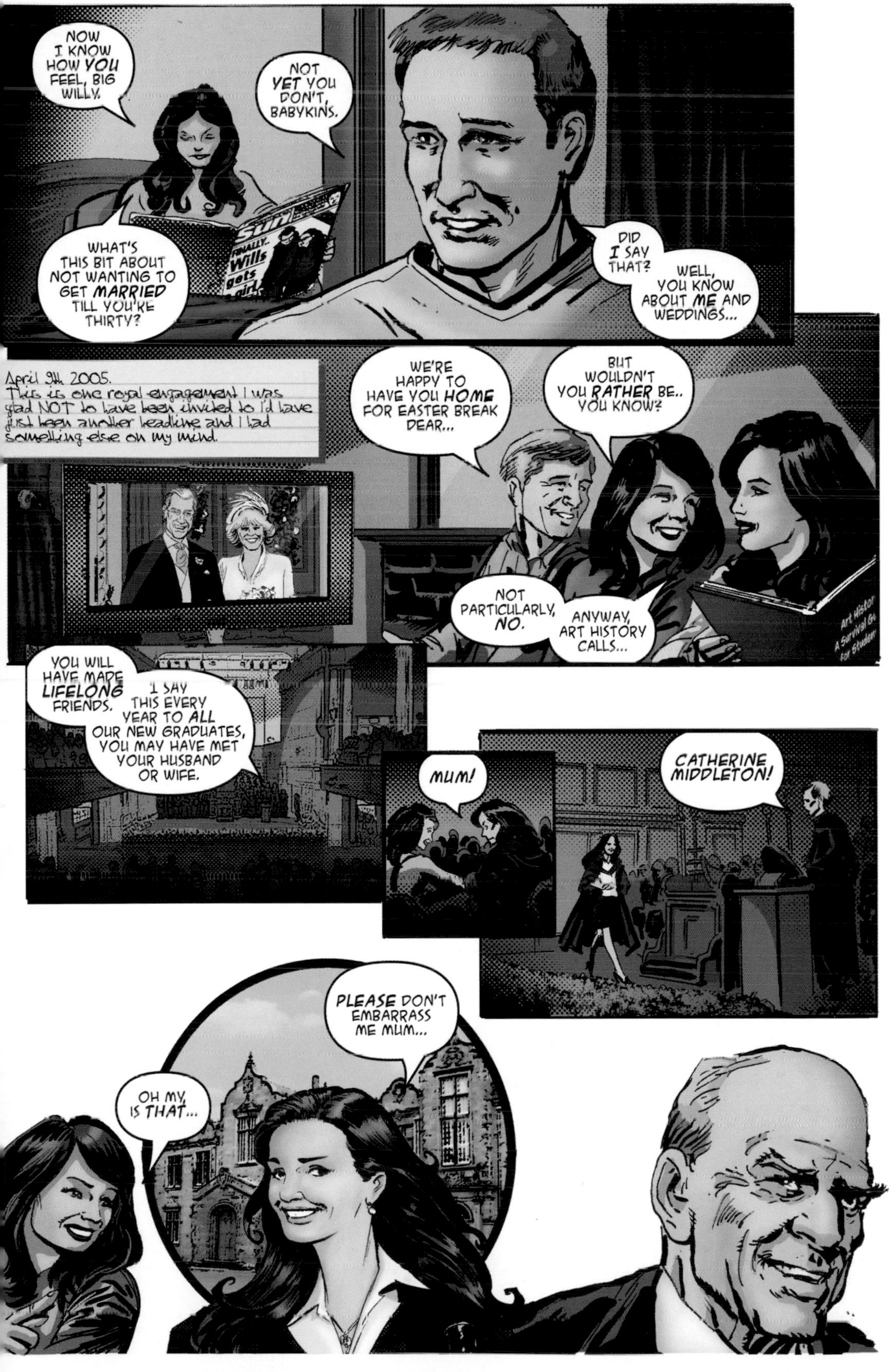
NOW I KNOW HOW YOU FEEL, BIG WILLY.
NOT YET YOU DON'T, BABYKINS.
Sun FINALLY... Wills gets girl
WHAT'S THIS BIT ABOUT NOT WANTING TO GET MARRIED TILL YOU'RE THIRTY?
DID I SAY THAT?
WELL, YOU KNOW ABOUT ME AND WEDDINGS...
April 9th 2005.
This is one royal engagement I was glad NOT to have been invited to I'd have just been another headline and I had something else on my mind.
WE'RE HAPPY TO HAVE YOU HOME FOR EASTER BREAK DEAR...
BUT WOULDN'T YOU RATHER BE.. YOU KNOW?
NOT PARTICULARLY, NO.
ANYWAY, ART HISTORY CALLS...
YOU WILL HAVE MADE LIFELONG FRIENDS.
I SAY THIS EVERY YEAR TO ALL OUR NEW GRADUATES, YOU MAY HAVE MET YOUR HUSBAND OR WIFE.
MUM!
CATHERINE MIDDLETON!
PLEASE DON'T EMBARRASS ME MUM...
OH MY, IS THAT...

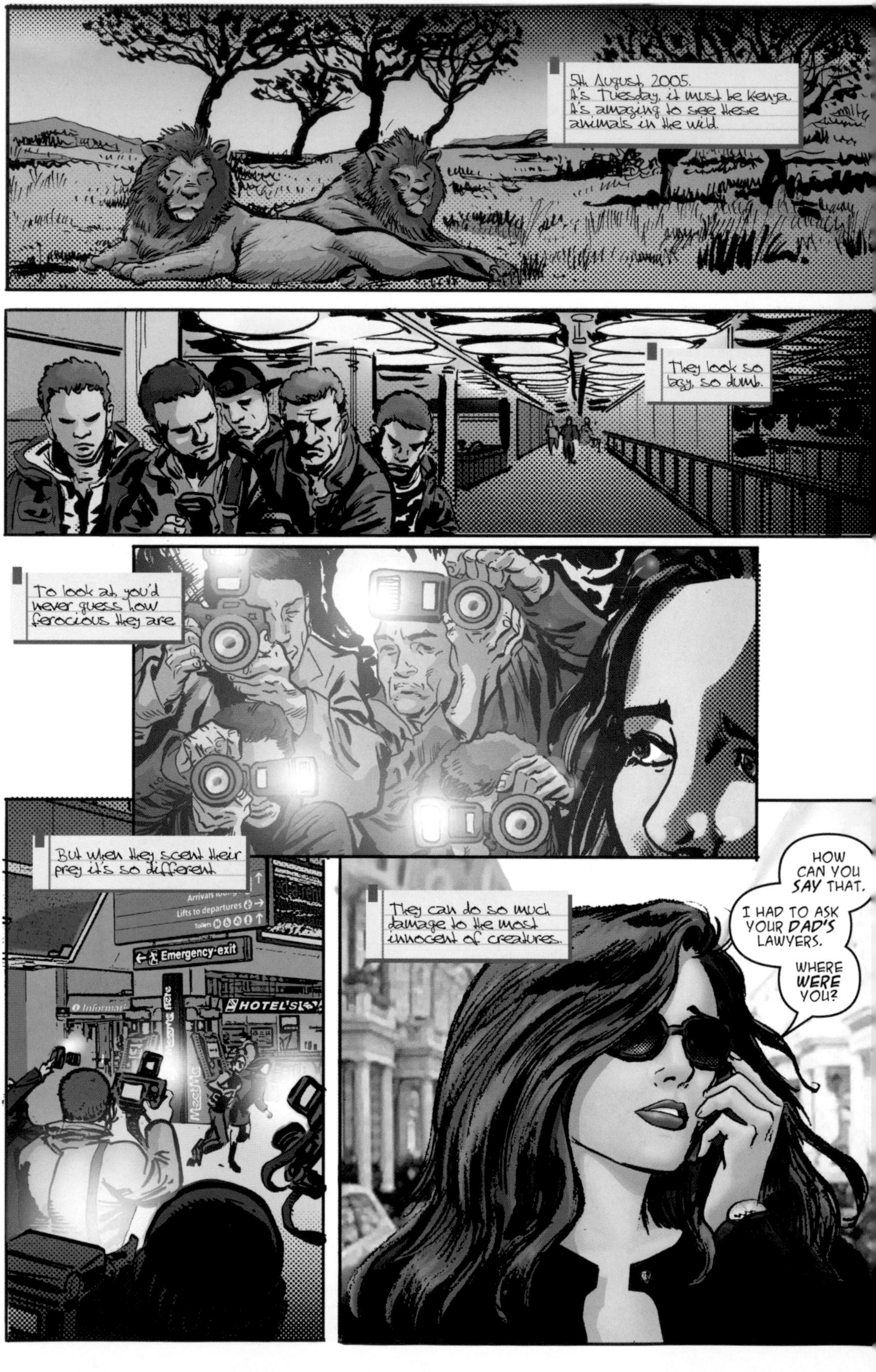

5th August, 2005.
It's Tuesday, it must be Kenya.
It's amazing to see these animals in the wild.
They look so lazy, so dumb.
To look at, you'd never guess how ferocious they are
But when they scent their prey it's so different
Arrivals
Lifts to departures
Toilets
Emergency-exit
HOTEL'S
They can do so much damage to the most innocent of creatures.
HOW CAN YOU SAY THAT.
I HAD TO ASK YOUR DAD'S LAWYERS.
WHERE WERE YOU?

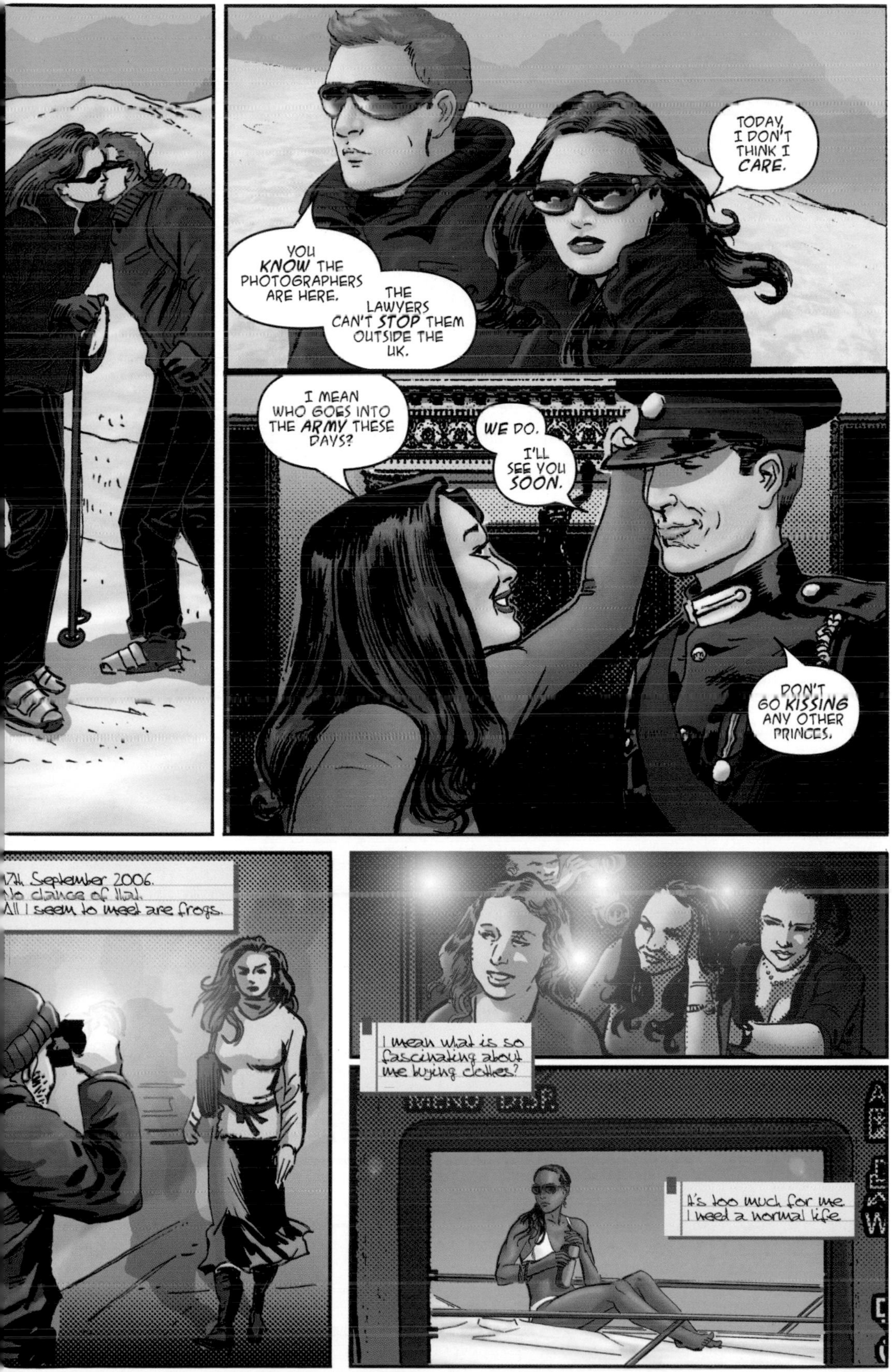
TODAY, I DON'T THINK I CARE.
YOU KNOW THE PHOTOGRAPHERS ARE HERE.
THE LAWYERS CAN'T STOP THEM OUTSIDE THE UK.
I MEAN WHO GOES INTO THE ARMY THESE DAYS?
WE DO.
I'LL SEE YOU SOON.
DON'T GO KISSING ANY OTHER PRINCES.
7th September 2006.
No chance of that.
All I seem to meet are frogs.
I mean what is so fascinating about me buying clothes?
It's too much for me.
I need a normal life.

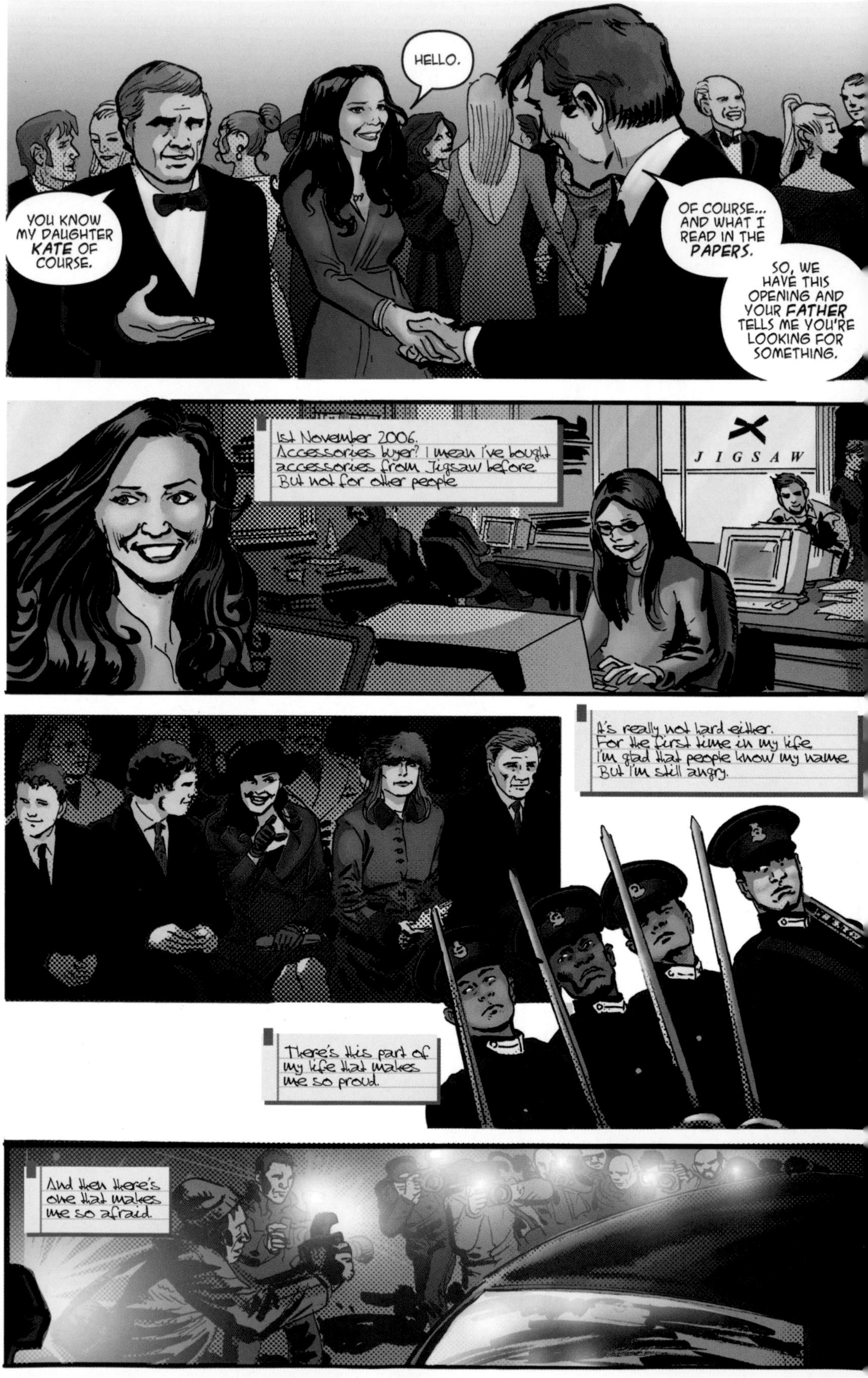
HELLO.
YOU KNOW MY DAUGHTER KATE OF COURSE.
OF COURSE... AND WHAT I READ IN THE PAPERS.
SO, WE HAVE THIS OPENING AND YOUR FATHER TELLS ME YOU'RE LOOKING FOR SOMETHING.
1st November 2006. Accessories buyer? I mean I've bought accessories from Jigsaw before. But not for other people.
JIGSAW
It's really not hard either. For the first time in my life, I'm glad that people know my name. But I'm still angry.
There's this part of my life that makes me so proud.
And then there's one that makes me so afraid.

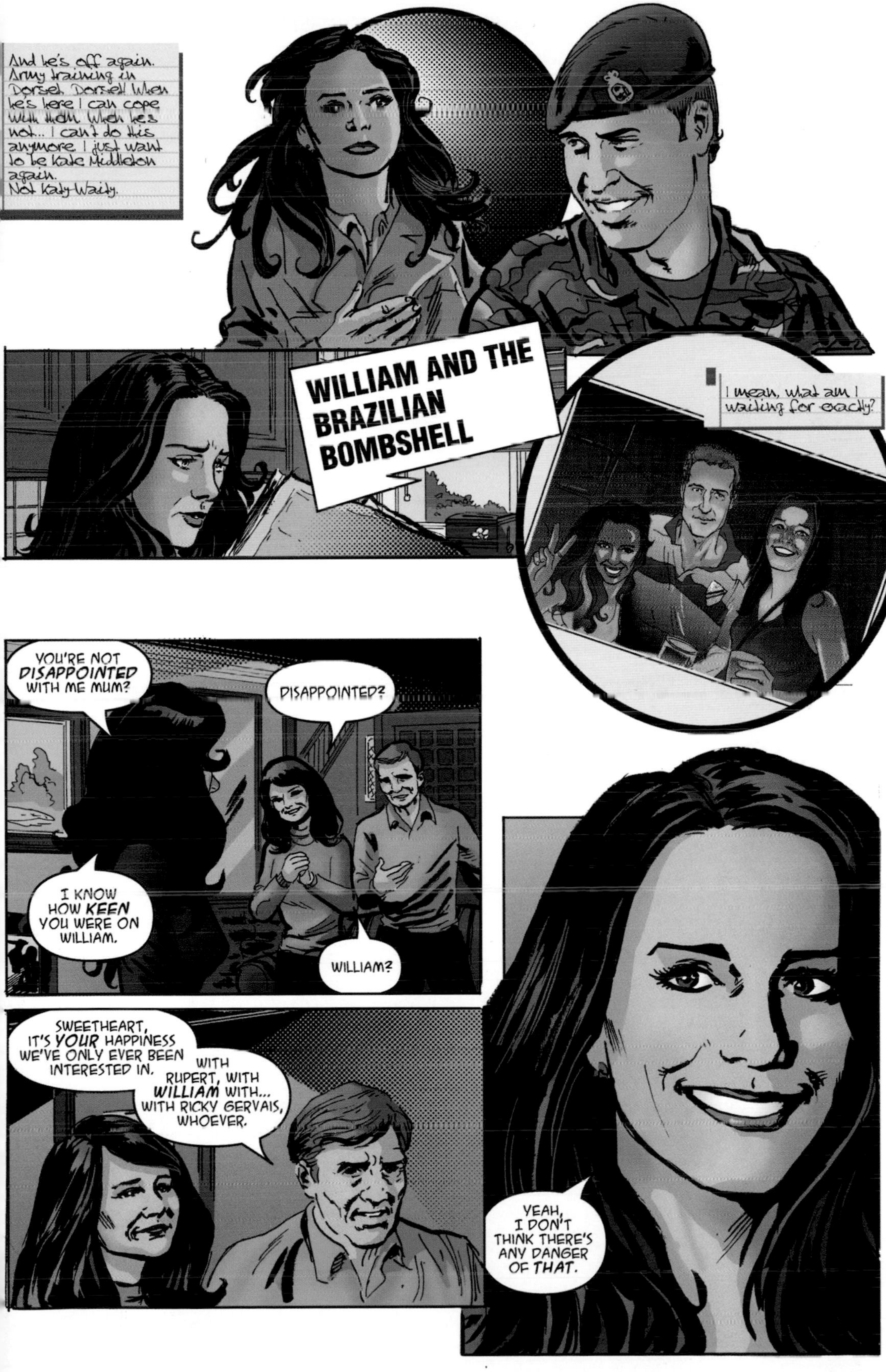

And he's off again. Army training in Dorset. Dorset! When he's here I can cope with them. When he's not... I can't do this anymore. I just want to be Kate Middleton again. Not Katy Waity.
WILLIAM AND THE BRAZILIAN BOMBSHELL
I mean, what am I waiting for exactly?
YOU'RE NOT DISAPPOINTED WITH ME MUM?
DISAPPOINTED?
I KNOW HOW KEEN YOU WERE ON WILLIAM.
WILLIAM?
SWEETHEART, IT'S YOUR HAPPINESS WE'VE ONLY EVER BEEN INTERESTED IN.
WITH RUPERT, WITH WILLIAM WITH... WITH RICKY GERVAIS, WHOEVER.
YEAH, I DON'T THINK THERE'S ANY DANGER OF THAT.

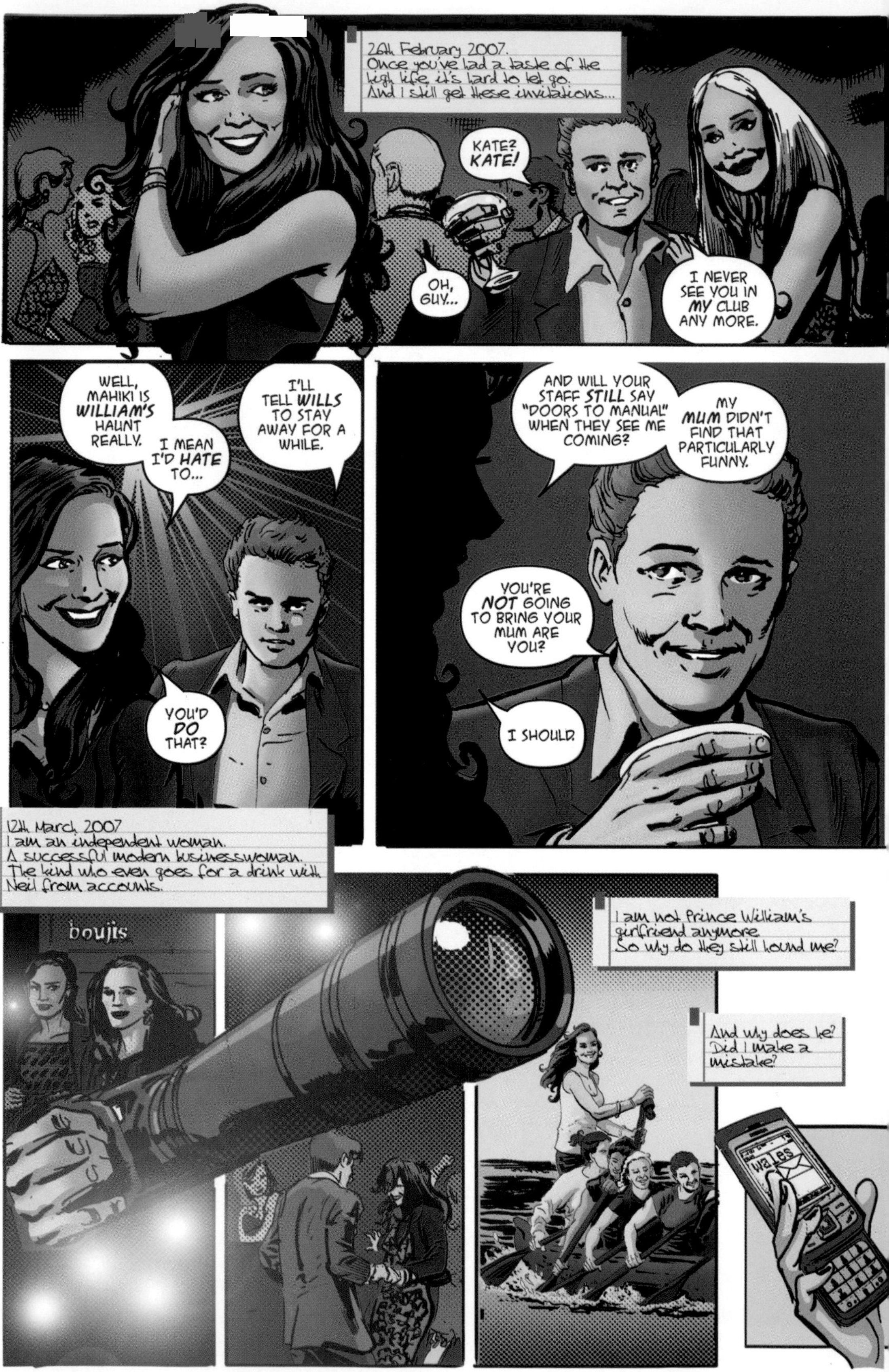
26th February 2007.
Once you've had a taste of the high life, it's hard to let go.
And I still get these invitations...
KATE? KATE!
OH, GUY...
I NEVER SEE YOU IN MY CLUB ANY MORE.
WELL, MAHIKI IS WILLIAM'S HAUNT REALLY.
I MEAN I'D HATE TO...
I'LL TELL WILLS TO STAY AWAY FOR A WHILE.
YOU'D DO THAT?
AND WILL YOUR STAFF STILL SAY "DOORS TO MANUAL" WHEN THEY SEE ME COMING?
MY MUM DIDN'T FIND THAT PARTICULARLY FUNNY.
YOU'RE NOT GOING TO BRING YOUR MUM ARE YOU?
I SHOULD.
12th March 2007
I am an independent woman.
A successful modern businesswoman.
The kind who even goes for a drink with Neil from accounts.
boujis
I am not Prince William's girlfriend anymore.
So why do they still hound me?
And why does he?
Did I make a mistake?
Wales

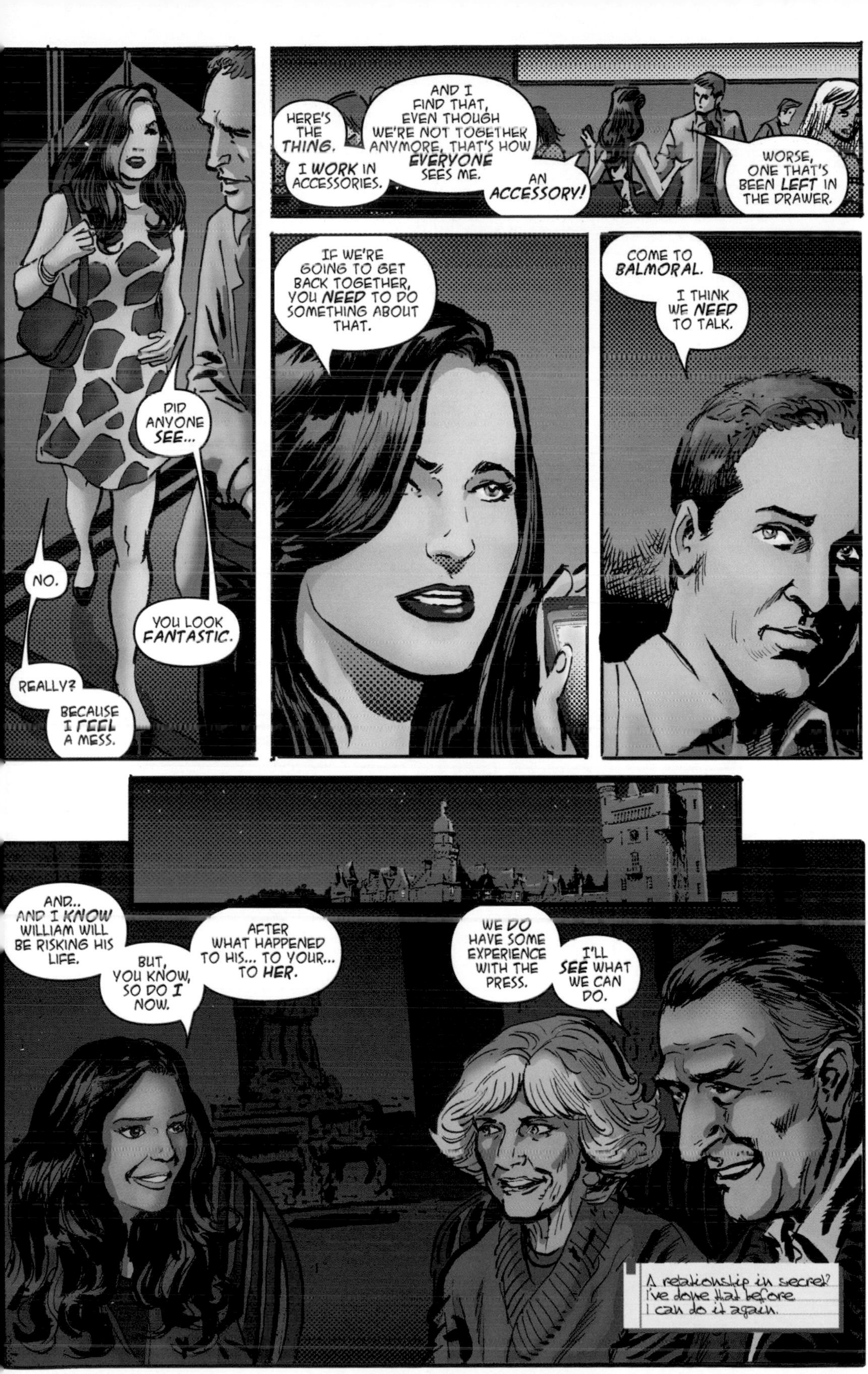
DID ANYONE SEE...
NO.
YOU LOOK FANTASTIC.
REALLY?
BECAUSE I FEEL A MESS.
HERE'S THE THING.
I WORK IN ACCESSORIES.
AND I FIND THAT, EVEN THOUGH WE'RE NOT TOGETHER ANYMORE, THAT'S HOW EVERYONE SEES ME.
AN ACCESSORY!
WORSE, ONE THAT'S BEEN LEFT IN THE DRAWER.
IF WE'RE GOING TO GET BACK TOGETHER, YOU NEED TO DO SOMETHING ABOUT THAT.
COME TO BALMORAL.
I THINK WE NEED TO TALK.
AND... AND I KNOW WILLIAM WILL BE RISKING HIS LIFE.
BUT, YOU KNOW, SO DO I NOW.
AFTER WHAT HAPPENED TO HIS... TO YOUR... TO HER.
WE DO HAVE SOME EXPERIENCE WITH THE PRESS.
I'LL SEE WHAT WE CAN DO.
A relationship in secret? I've done that before. I can do it again.

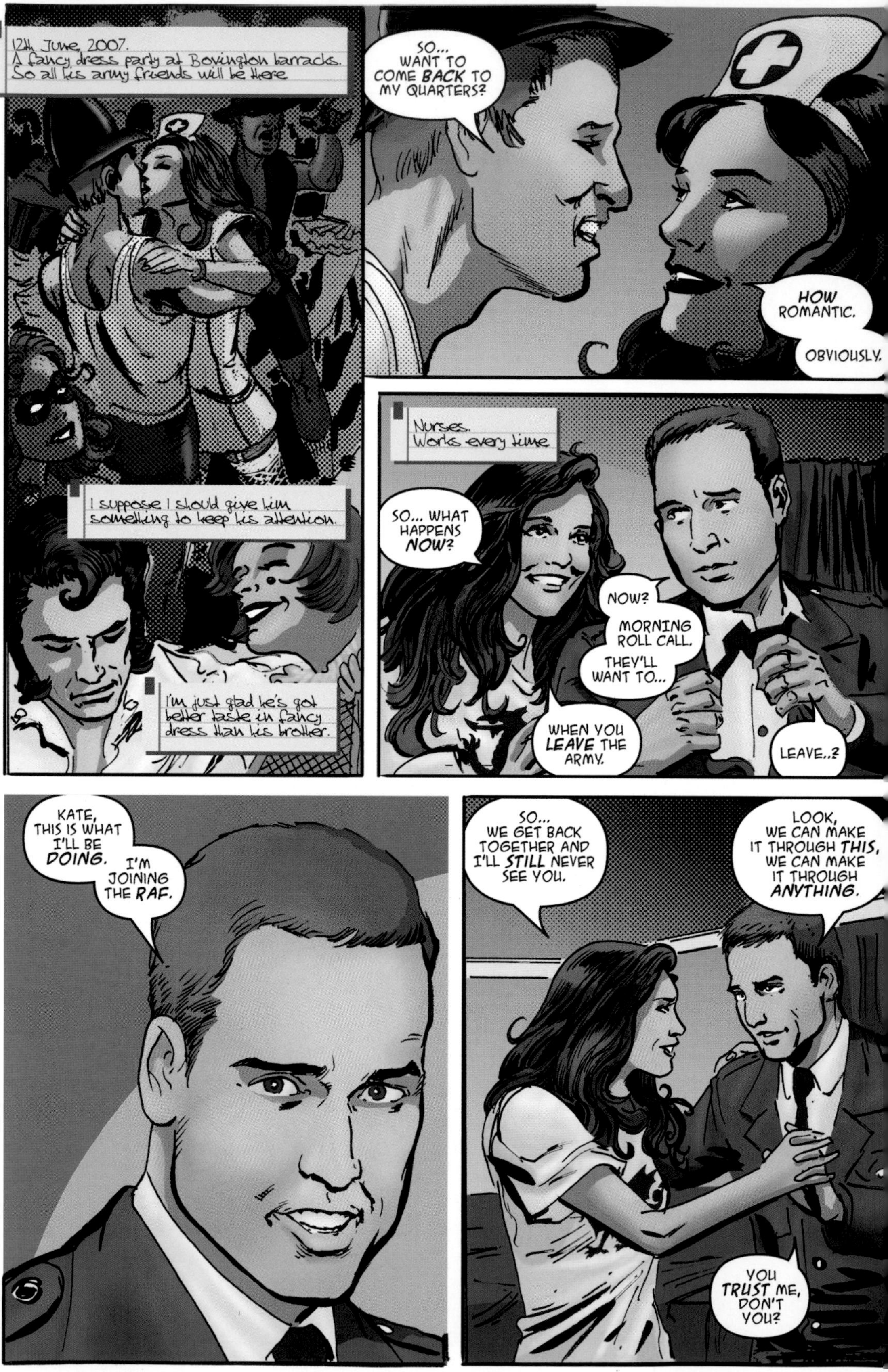
12th June, 2007.
A fancy dress party at Bovington barracks.
So all his army friends will be there
I suppose I should give him something to keep his attention.
I'm just glad he's got better taste in fancy dress than his brother.
SO... WANT TO COME BACK TO MY QUARTERS?
HOW ROMANTIC.
OBVIOUSLY.
Nurses.
Works every time
SO... WHAT HAPPENS NOW?
NOW?
MORNING ROLL CALL.
THEY'LL WANT TO...
WHEN YOU LEAVE THE ARMY.
LEAVE..?
KATE, THIS IS WHAT I'LL BE DOING.
I'M JOINING THE RAF.
SO... WE GET BACK TOGETHER AND I'LL STILL NEVER SEE YOU.
LOOK, WE CAN MAKE IT THROUGH THIS, WE CAN MAKE IT THROUGH ANYTHING.
YOU TRUST ME, DON'T YOU?

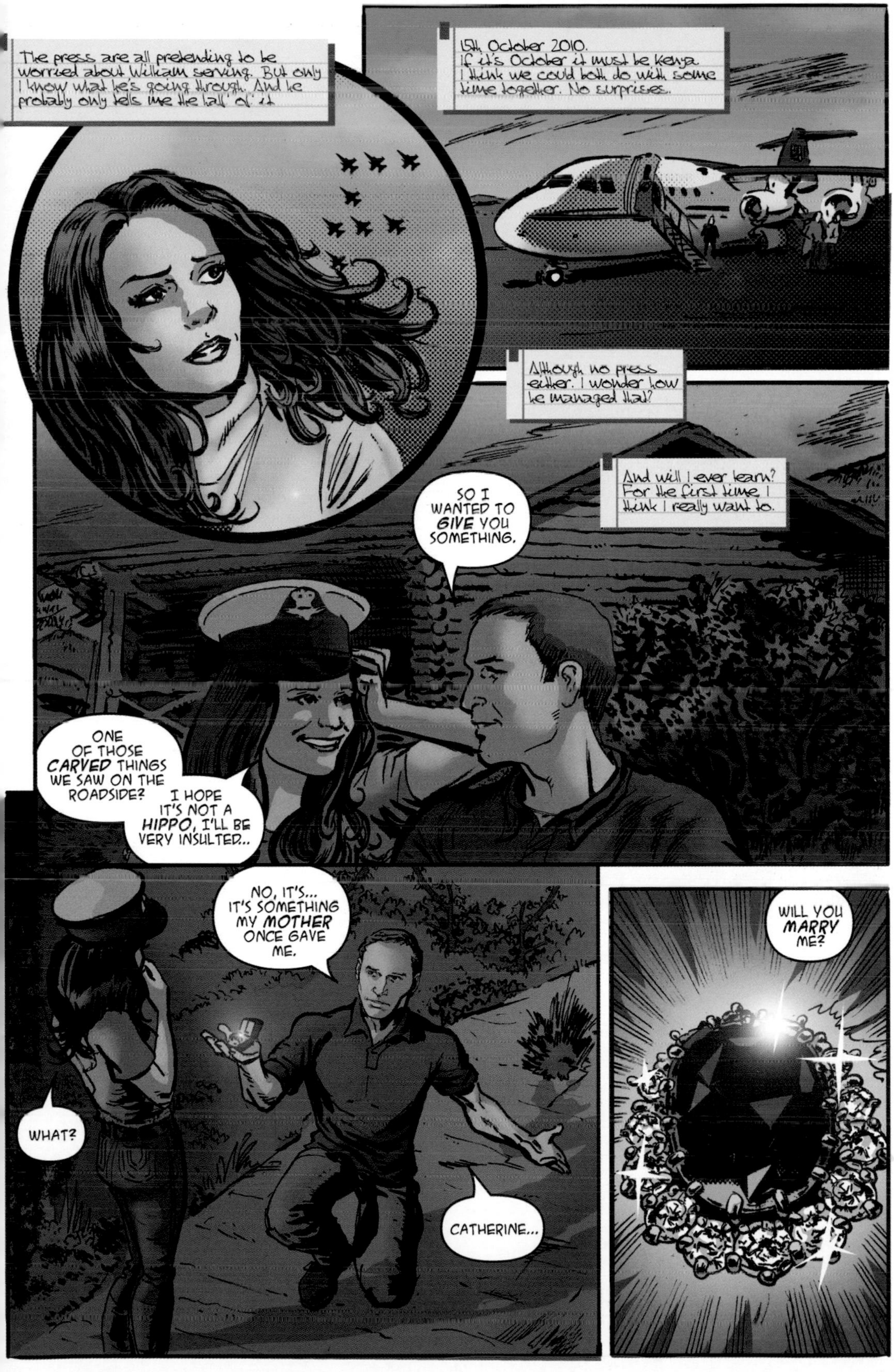

The press are all pretending to be worried about William serving. But only I know what he's going through. And he probably only tells me the half of it
15th October 2010.
If it's October it must be Kenya.
I think we could both do with some time together. No surprises.
Although no press either. I wonder how he managed that?
And will I ever learn? For the first time I think I really want to.
SO I WANTED TO GIVE YOU SOMETHING.
ONE OF THOSE CARVED THINGS WE SAW ON THE ROADSIDE?
I HOPE IT'S NOT A HIPPO, I'LL BE VERY INSULTED...
NO, IT'S... IT'S SOMETHING MY MOTHER ONCE GAVE ME.
WHAT?
CATHERINE...
WILL YOU MARRY ME?

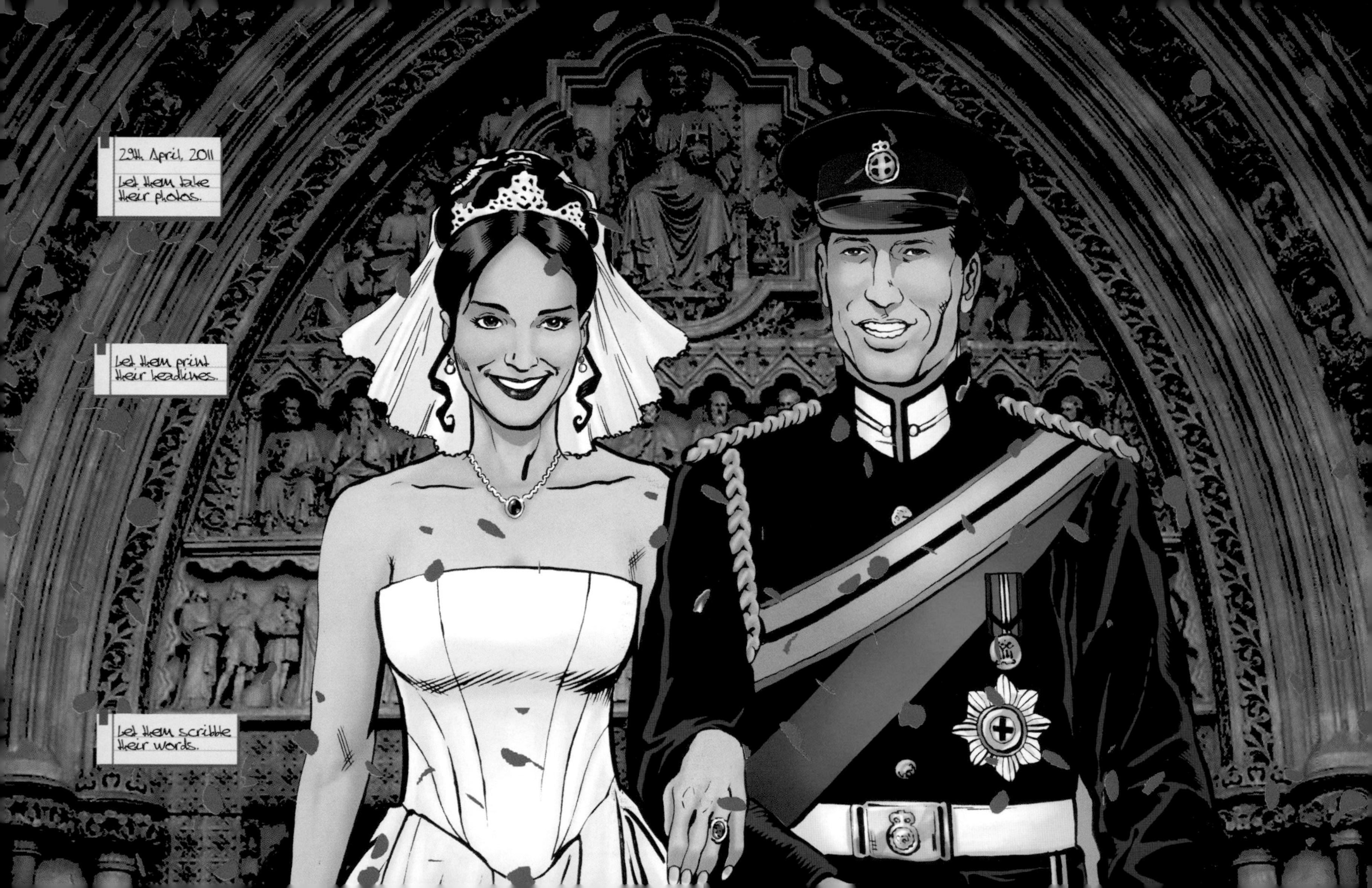
29th April, 2011
Let them take their photos.
Let them print their headlines.
Let them scribble their words.

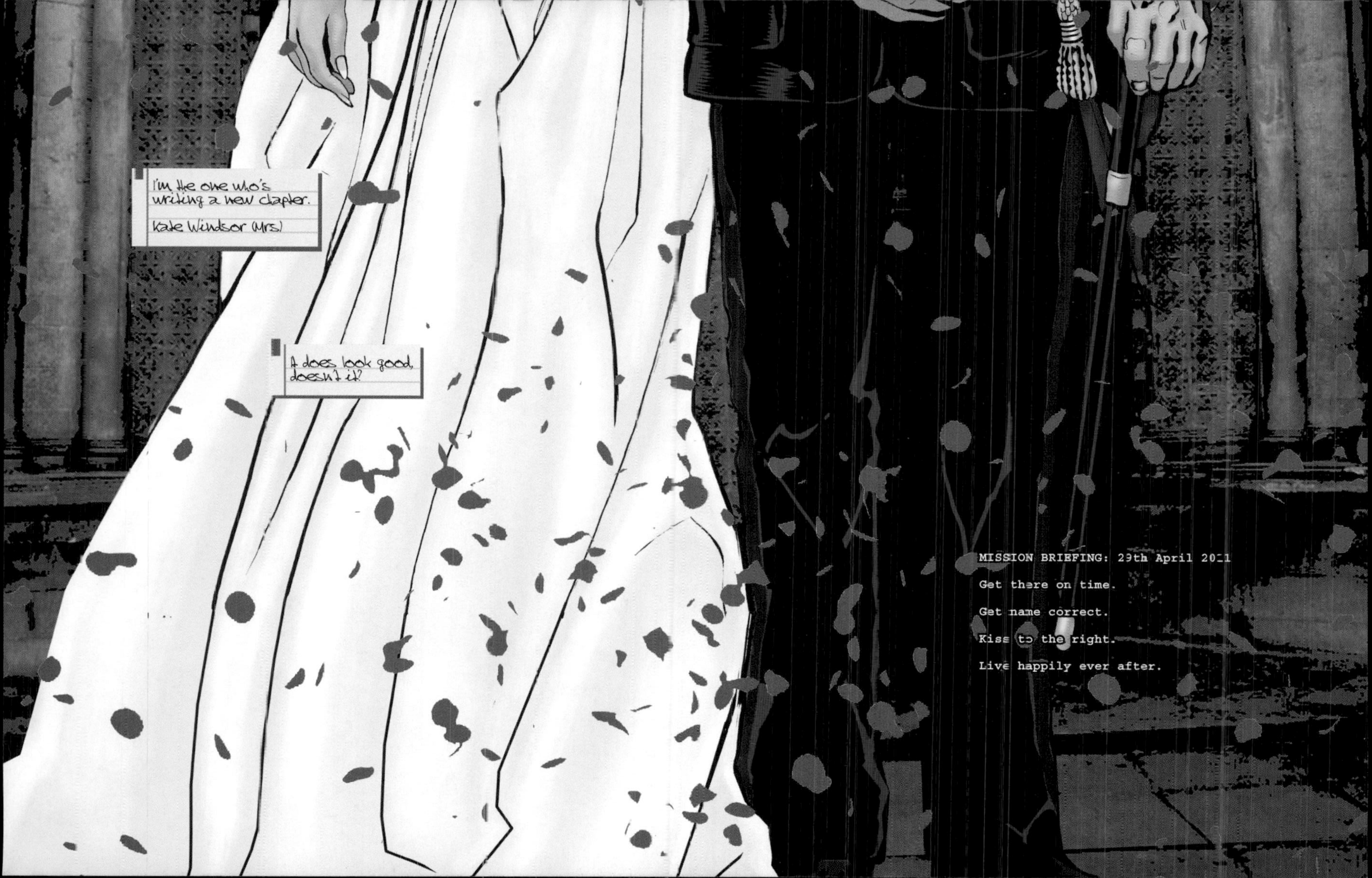

I'm the one who's writing a new chapter.
Kate Windsor (Mrs)
It does look good, doesn't it?
MISSION BRIEFING: 29th April 2011
Get there on time.
Get name correct.
Kiss to the right.
Live happily ever after.

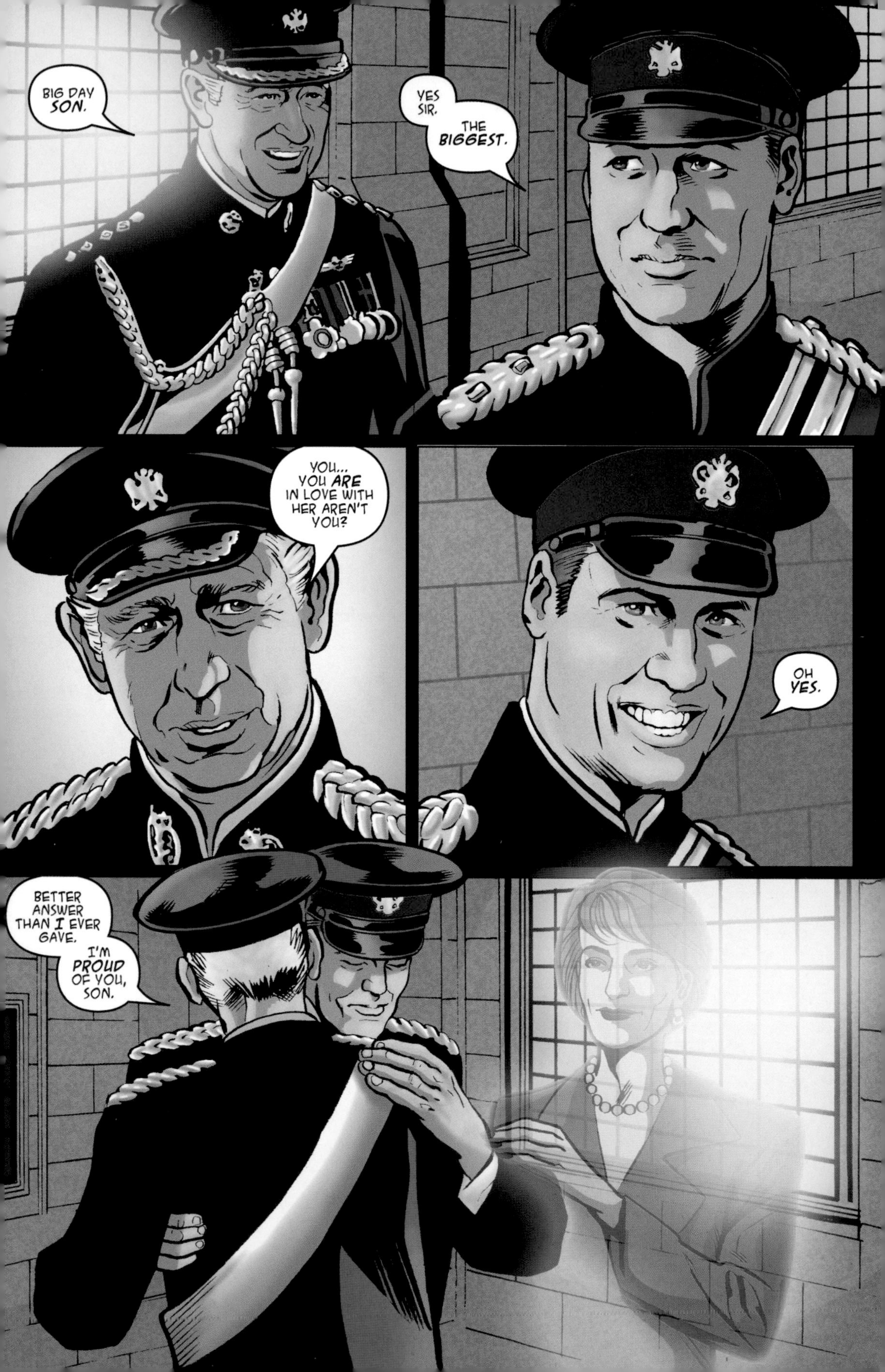
BIG DAY SON.
YES SIR.
THE BIGGEST.
YOU... YOU ARE IN LOVE WITH HER AREN'T YOU?
OH YES.
BETTER ANSWER THAN I EVER GAVE.
I'M PROUD OF YOU, SON.

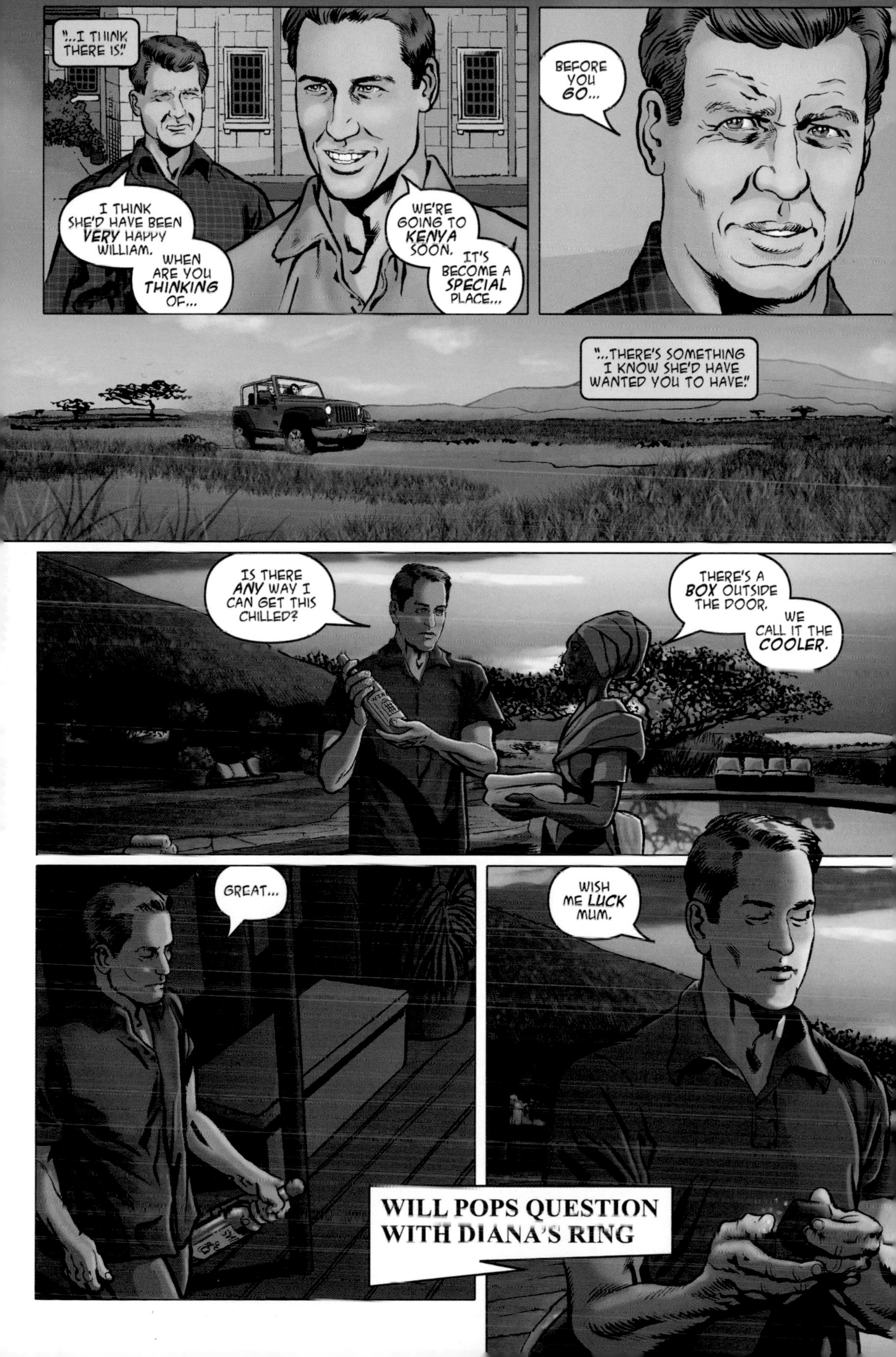
"...I THINK THERE IS."
I THINK SHE'D HAVE BEEN VERY HAPPY WILLIAM.
WHEN ARE YOU THINKING OF...
WE'RE GOING TO KENYA SOON.
IT'S BECOME A SPECIAL PLACE...
BEFORE YOU GO...
"...THERE'S SOMETHING I KNOW SHE'D HAVE WANTED YOU TO HAVE."
IS THERE ANY WAY I CAN GET THIS CHILLED?
THERE'S A BOX OUTSIDE THE DOOR.
WE CALL IT THE COOLER.
GREAT...
WISH ME LUCK MUM.
WILL POPS QUESTION WITH DIANA'S RING

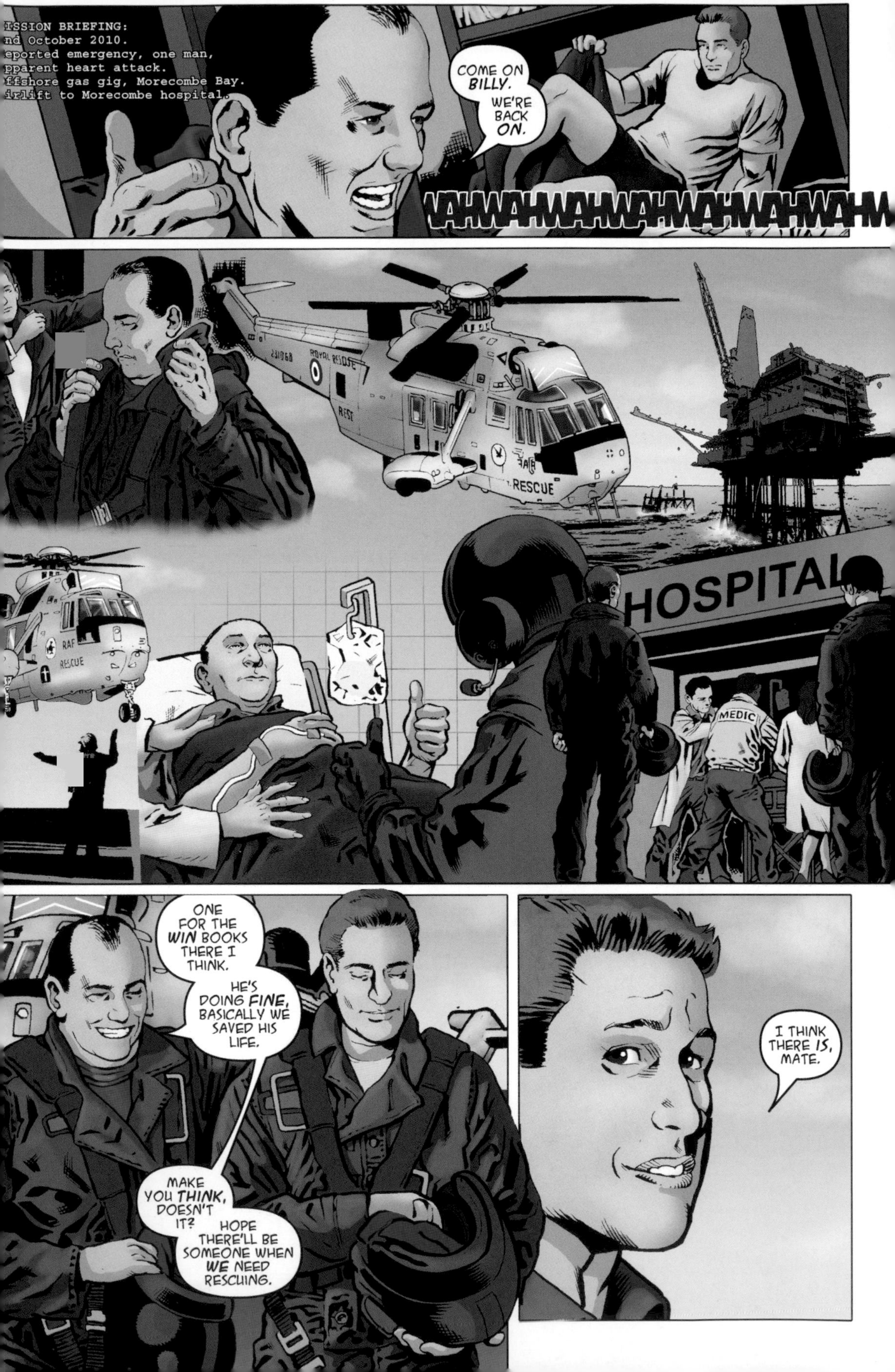
ISSION BRIEFING:
nd October 2010.
eported emergency, one man,
pparent heart attack.
ffshore gas gig, Morecombe Bay.
irlift to Morecombe hospital.
COME ON BILLY.
WE'RE BACK ON.
WAHWAHWAHWAHWAHWAHWAHWAHM
ROYAL RESCUE
RAF
RESCUE
HOSPITAL
MEDIC
ONE FOR THE WIN BOOKS THERE I THINK.
HE'S DOING FINE, BASICALLY WE SAVED HIS LIFE.
MAKE YOU THINK, DOESN'T IT?
HOPE THERE'LL BE SOMEONE WHEN WE NEED RESCUING.
I THINK THERE IS, MATE.

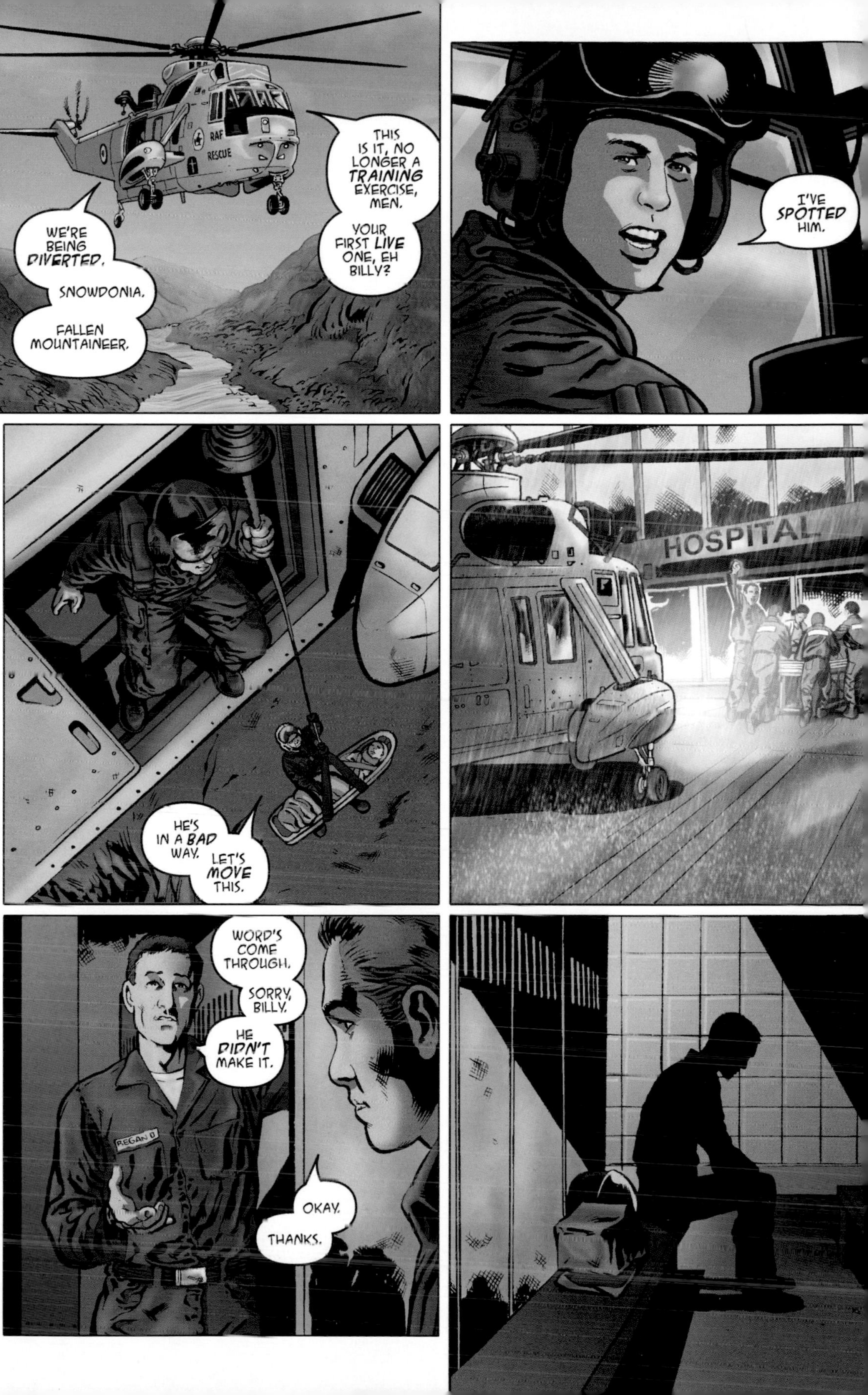

RAF
RESCUE
WE'RE BEING *DIVERTED*.
SNOWDONIA.
FALLEN MOUNTAINEER.
THIS IS IT, NO LONGER A *TRAINING* EXERCISE, MEN.
YOUR FIRST *LIVE* ONE, EH BILLY?
I'VE *SPOTTED* HIM.
HE'S IN A *BAD* WAY.
LET'S *MOVE* THIS.
HOSPITAL
WORD'S COME THROUGH.
SORRY, BILLY.
HE *DIDN'T* MAKE IT.
REGAN D.
OKAY.
THANKS.

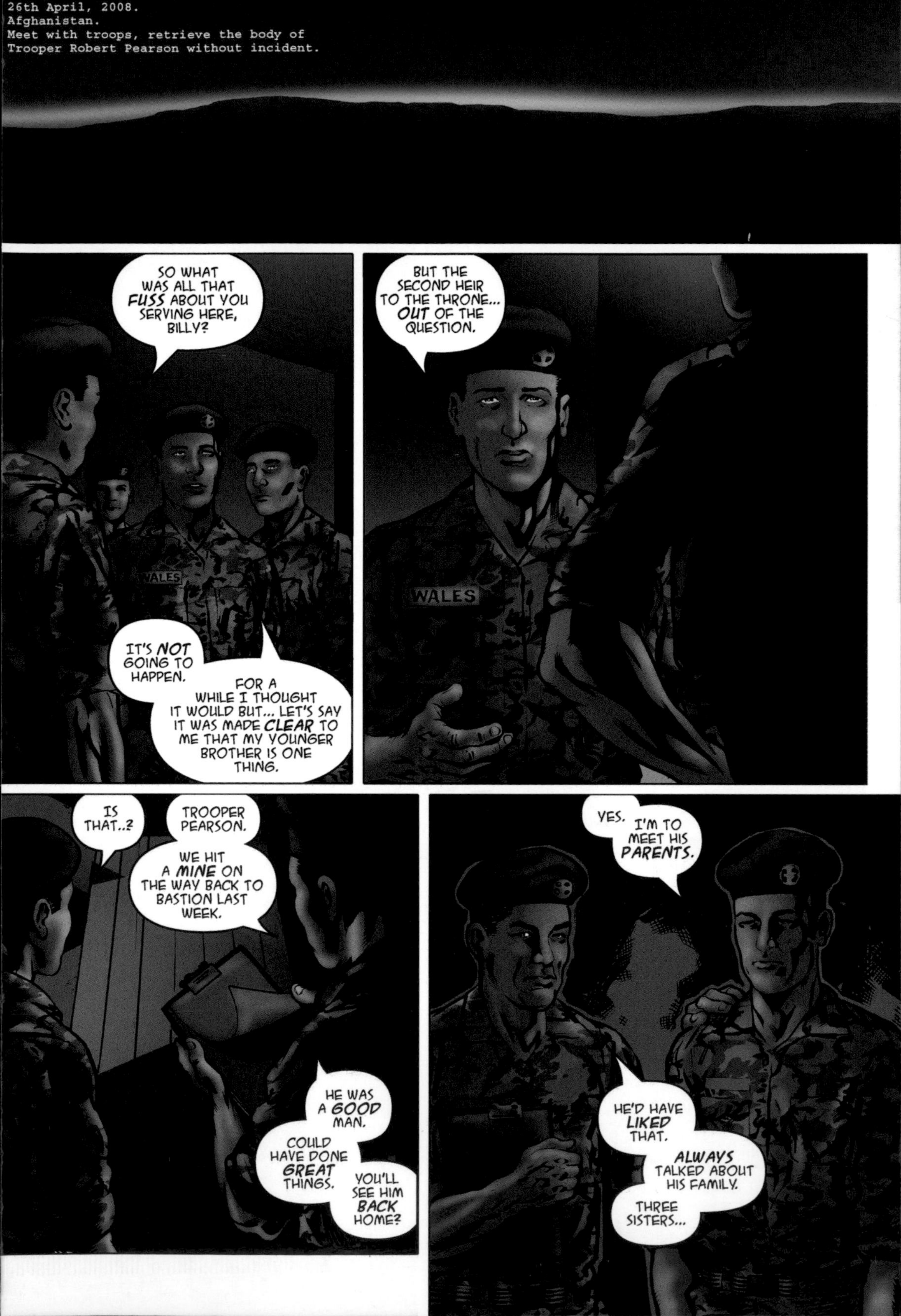
26th April, 2008.
Afghanistan.
Meet with troops, retrieve the body of
Trooper Robert Pearson without incident.
SO WHAT WAS ALL THAT FUSS ABOUT YOU SERVING HERE, BILLY?
WALES
IT'S NOT GOING TO HAPPEN.
FOR A WHILE I THOUGHT IT WOULD BUT... LET'S SAY IT WAS MADE CLEAR TO ME THAT MY YOUNGER BROTHER IS ONE THING.
BUT THE SECOND HEIR TO THE THRONE... OUT OF THE QUESTION.
WALES
IS THAT..?
TROOPER PEARSON.
WE HIT A MINE ON THE WAY BACK TO BASTION LAST WEEK.
HE WAS A GOOD MAN.
COULD HAVE DONE GREAT THINGS.
YOU'LL SEE HIM BACK HOME?
YES. I'M TO MEET HIS PARENTS.
HE'D HAVE LIKED THAT.
ALWAYS TALKED ABOUT HIS FAMILY.
THREE SISTERS...

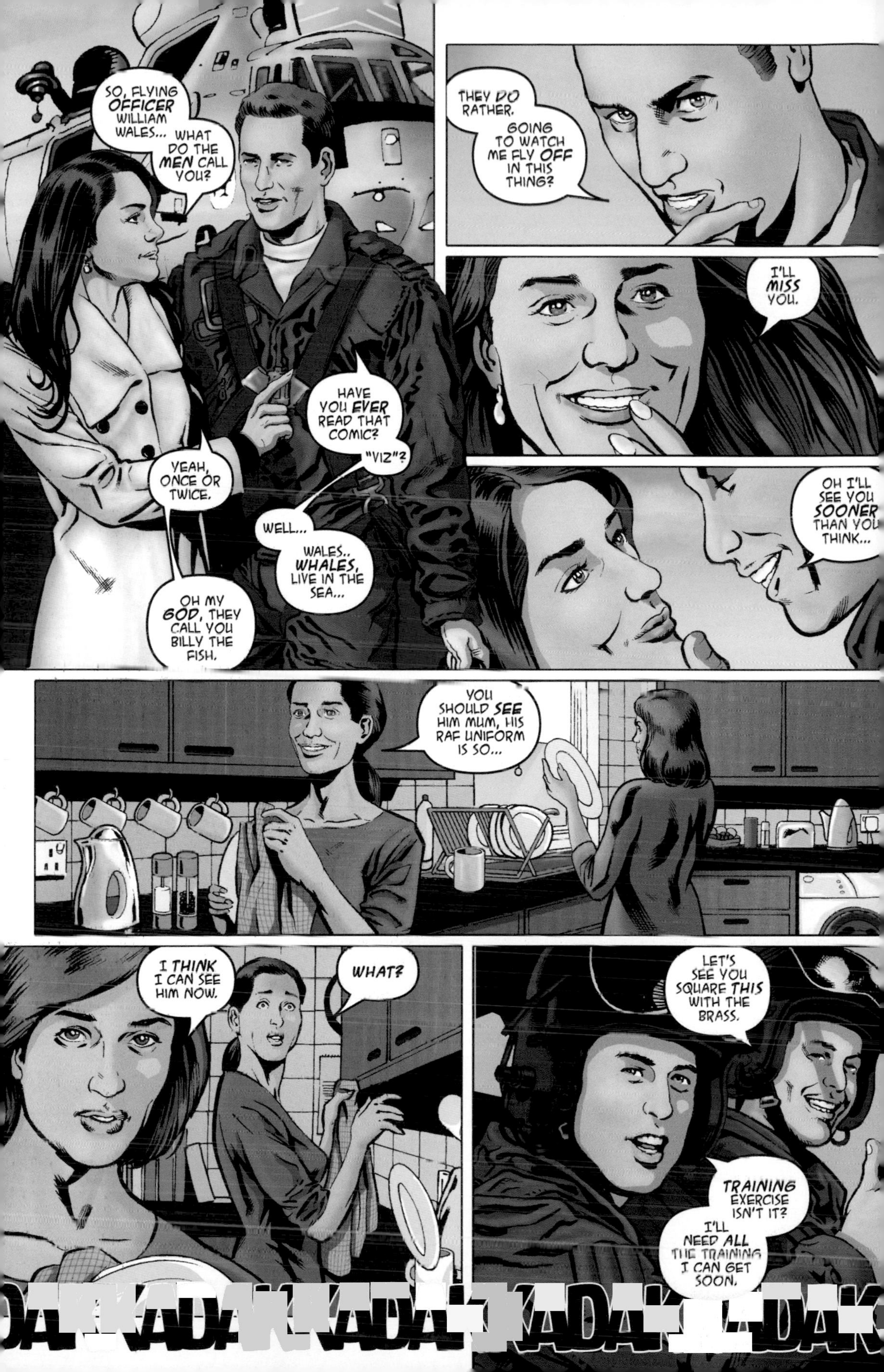

SO, FLYING OFFICER WILLIAM WALES... WHAT DO THE MEN CALL YOU?
HAVE YOU EVER READ THAT COMIC?
"VIZ"?
YEAH, ONCE OR TWICE.
WELL...
WALES.. WHALES, LIVE IN THE SEA...
OH MY GOD, THEY CALL YOU BILLY THE FISH.
THEY DO RATHER.
GOING TO WATCH ME FLY OFF IN THIS THING?
I'LL MISS YOU.
OH I'LL SEE YOU SOONER THAN YOU THINK...
YOU SHOULD SEE HIM MUM, HIS RAF UNIFORM IS SO...
I THINK I CAN SEE HIM NOW.
WHAT?
LET'S SEE YOU SQUARE THIS WITH THE BRASS.
TRAINING EXERCISE ISN'T IT?
I'LL NEED ALL THE TRAINING I CAN GET SOON.

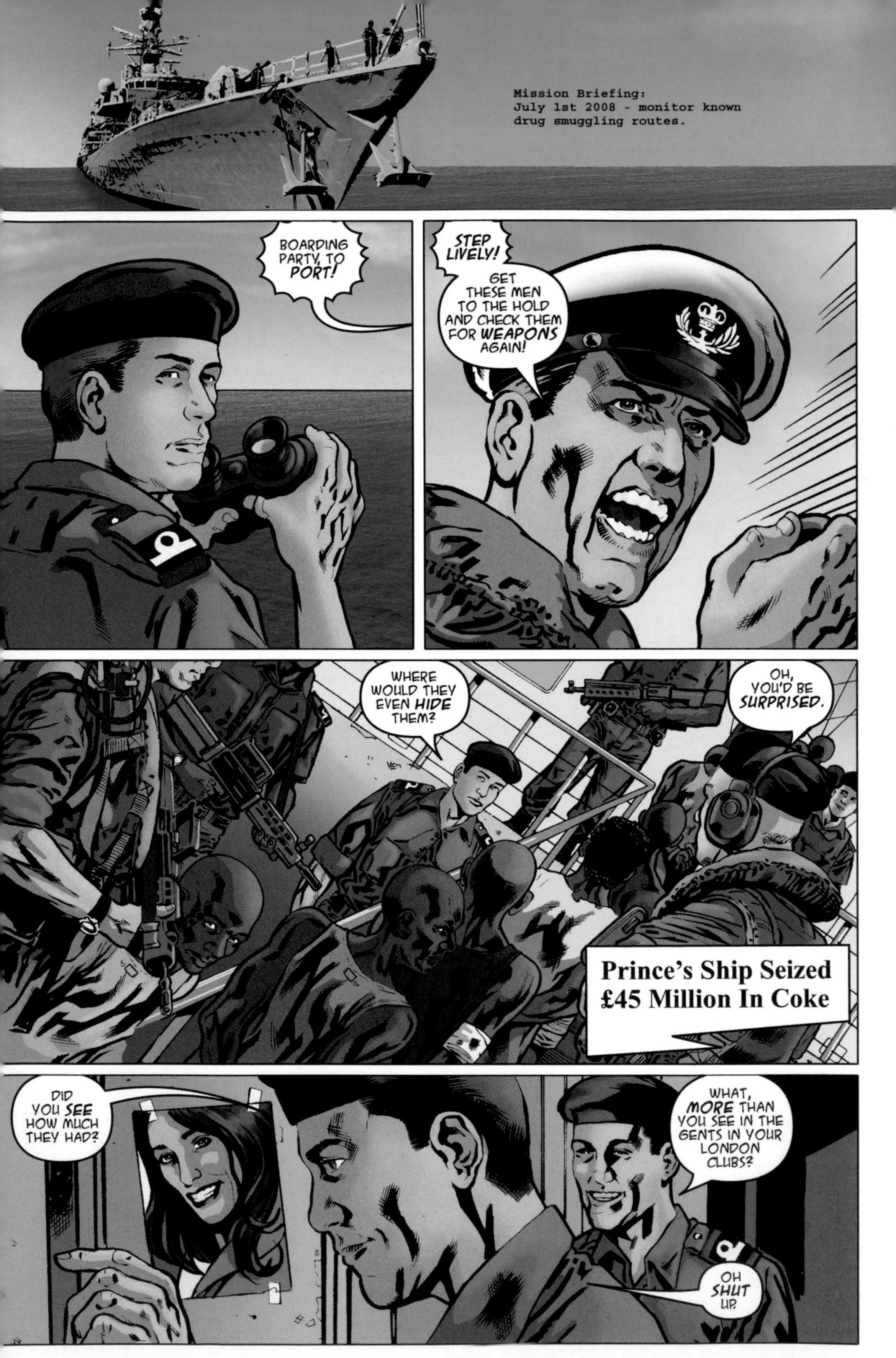
Mission Briefing:
July 1st 2008 - monitor known
drug smuggling routes.
BOARDING PARTY, TO PORT!
STEP LIVELY!
GET THESE MEN TO THE HOLD AND CHECK THEM FOR WEAPONS AGAIN!
WHERE WOULD THEY EVEN HIDE THEM?
OH, YOU'D BE SURPRISED.
Prince's Ship Seized
£45 Million In Coke
DID YOU SEE HOW MUCH THEY HAD?
WHAT, MORE THAN YOU SEE IN THE GENTS IN YOUR LONDON CLUBS?
OH SHUT UP.

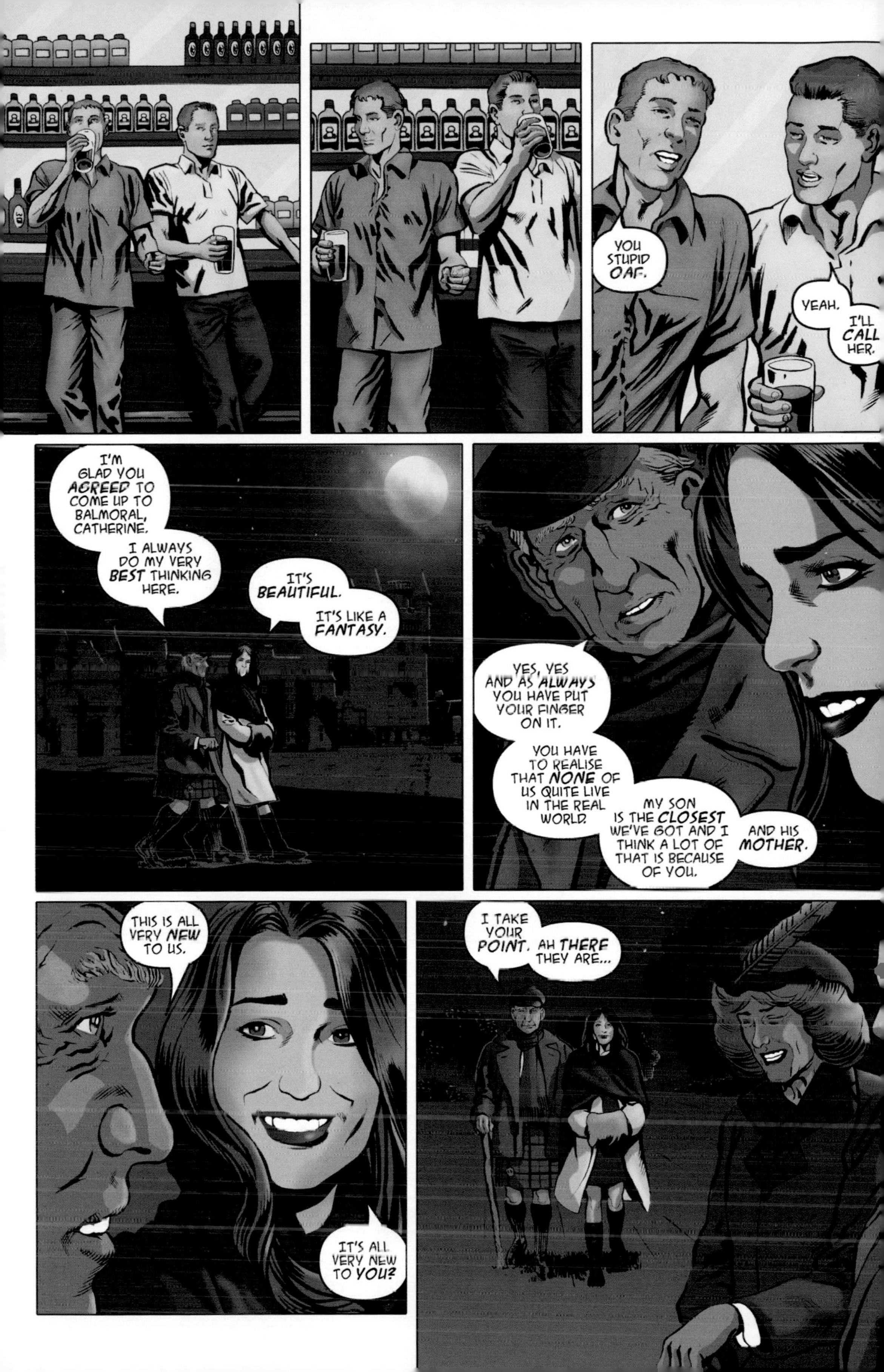
YOU STUPID OAF.
YEAH.
I'LL CALL HER.
I'M GLAD YOU AGREED TO COME UP TO BALMORAL, CATHERINE.
I ALWAYS DO MY VERY BEST THINKING HERE.
IT'S BEAUTIFUL.
IT'S LIKE A FANTASY.
YES, YES AND AS ALWAYS YOU HAVE PUT YOUR FINGER ON IT.
YOU HAVE TO REALISE THAT NONE OF US QUITE LIVE IN THE REAL WORLD.
MY SON IS THE CLOSEST WE'VE GOT AND I THINK A LOT OF THAT IS BECAUSE OF YOU.
AND HIS MOTHER.
THIS IS ALL VERY NEW TO US.
IT'S ALL VERY NEW TO YOU?
I TAKE YOUR POINT.
AH THERE THEY ARE...

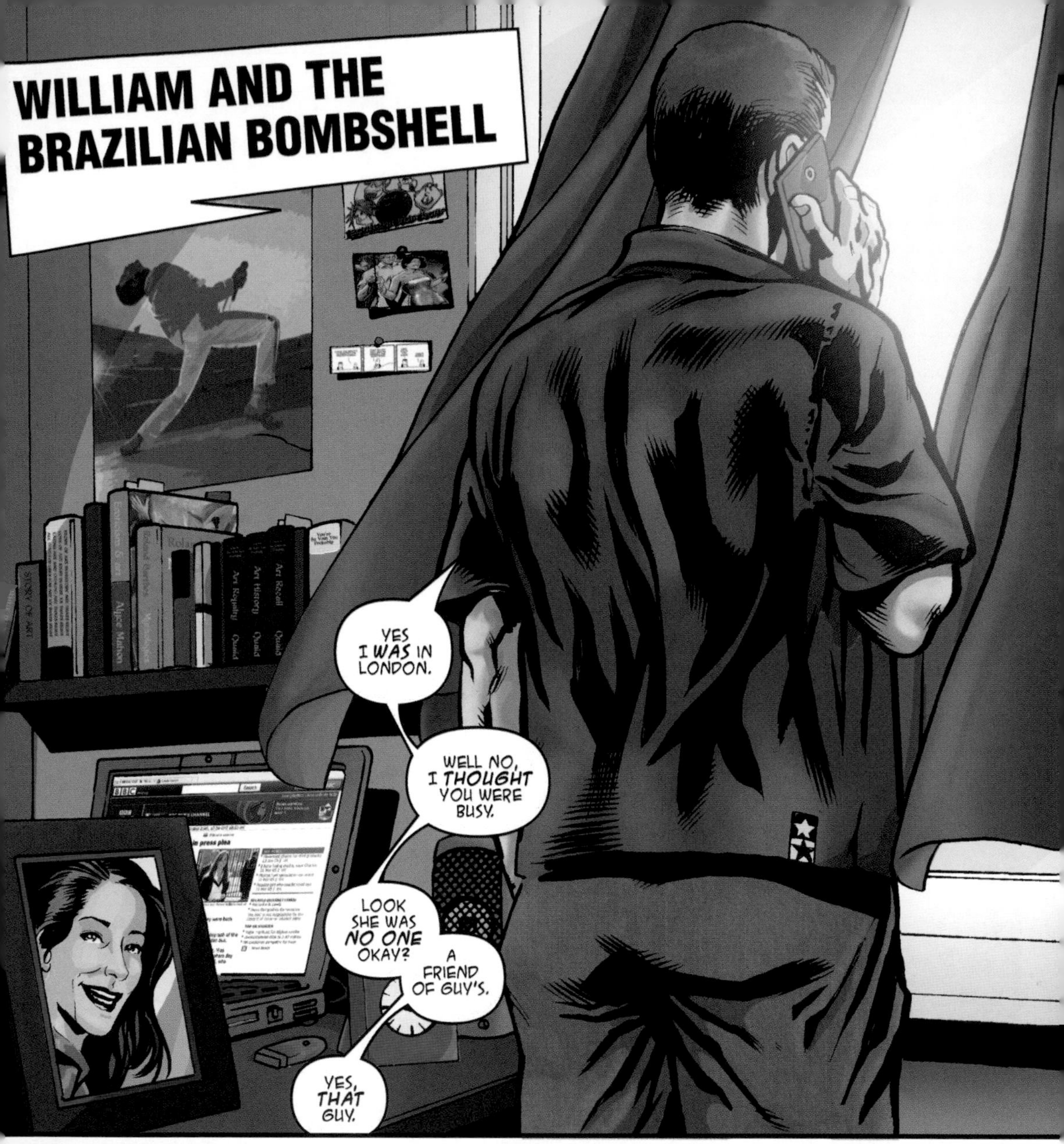
WILLIAM AND THE BRAZILIAN BOMBSHELL
YES I WAS IN LONDON.
WELL NO, I THOUGHT YOU WERE BUSY.
LOOK SHE WAS NO ONE OKAY?
A FRIEND OF GUY'S.
YES, THAT GUY.

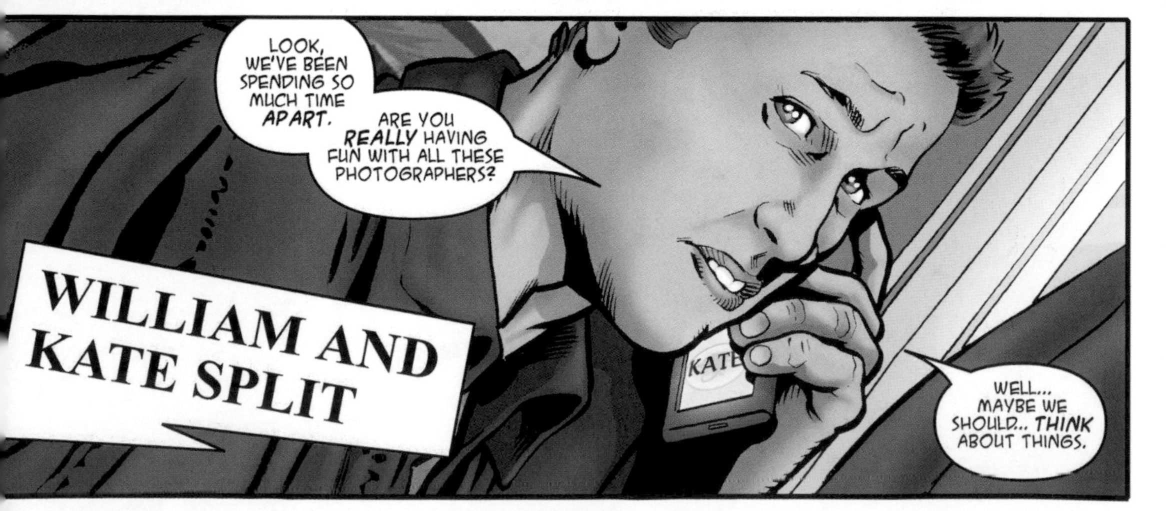
LOOK, WE'VE BEEN SPENDING SO MUCH TIME APART.
ARE YOU REALLY HAVING FUN WITH ALL THESE PHOTOGRAPHERS?
WILLIAM AND KATE SPLIT
KATE
WELL... MAYBE WE SHOULD... THINK ABOUT THINGS.

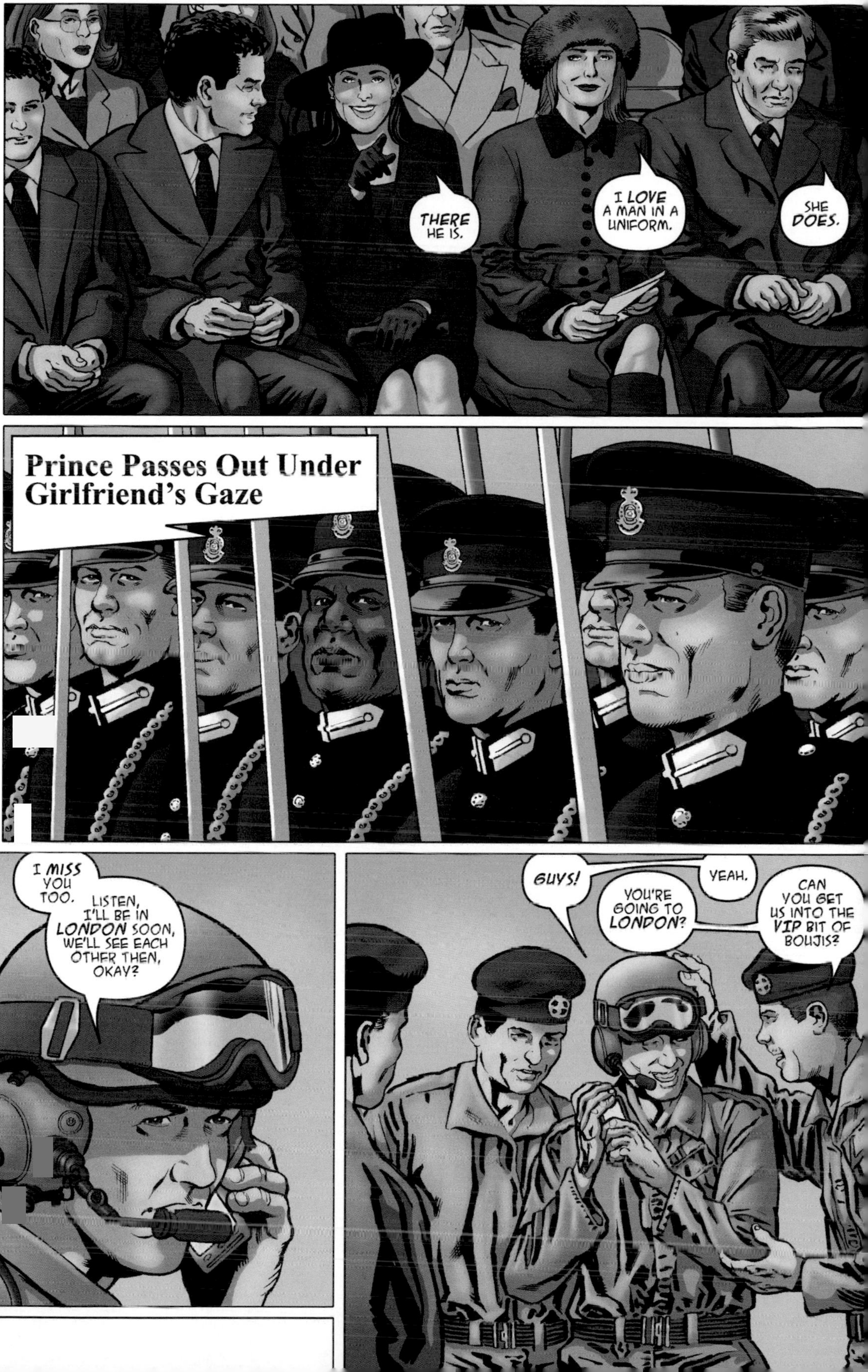
THERE HE IS.
I LOVE A MAN IN A UNIFORM.
SHE DOES.
Prince Passes Out Under Girlfriend's Gaze
I MISS YOU TOO.
LISTEN, I'LL BE IN LONDON SOON, WE'LL SEE EACH OTHER THEN, OKAY?
GUYS!
YEAH.
YOU'RE GOING TO LONDON?
CAN YOU GET US INTO THE VIP BIT OF BOUJIS?

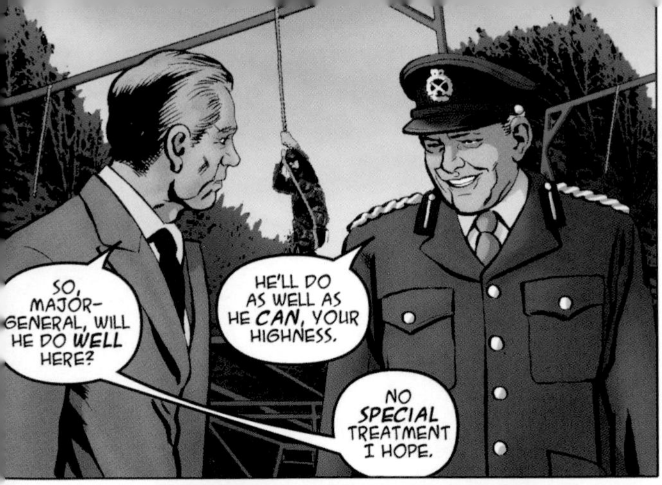
SO, MAJOR-GENERAL, WILL HE DO WELL HERE?
HE'LL DO AS WELL AS HE CAN, YOUR HIGHNESS.
NO SPECIAL TREATMENT I HOPE.

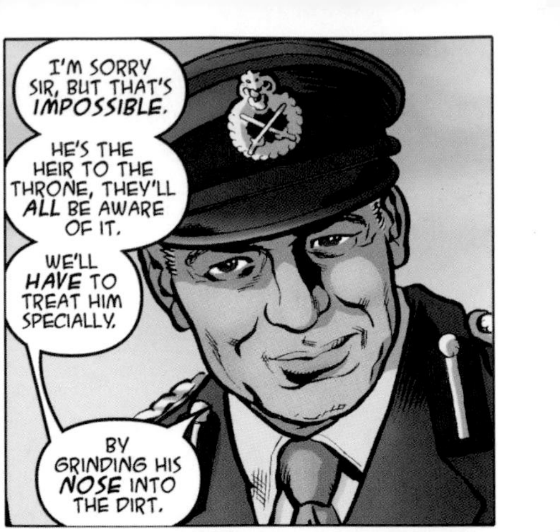
I'M SORRY SIR, BUT THAT'S IMPOSSIBLE.
HE'S THE HEIR TO THE THRONE, THEY'LL ALL BE AWARE OF IT.
WE'LL HAVE TO TREAT HIM SPECIALLY.
BY GRINDING HIS NOSE INTO THE DIRT.

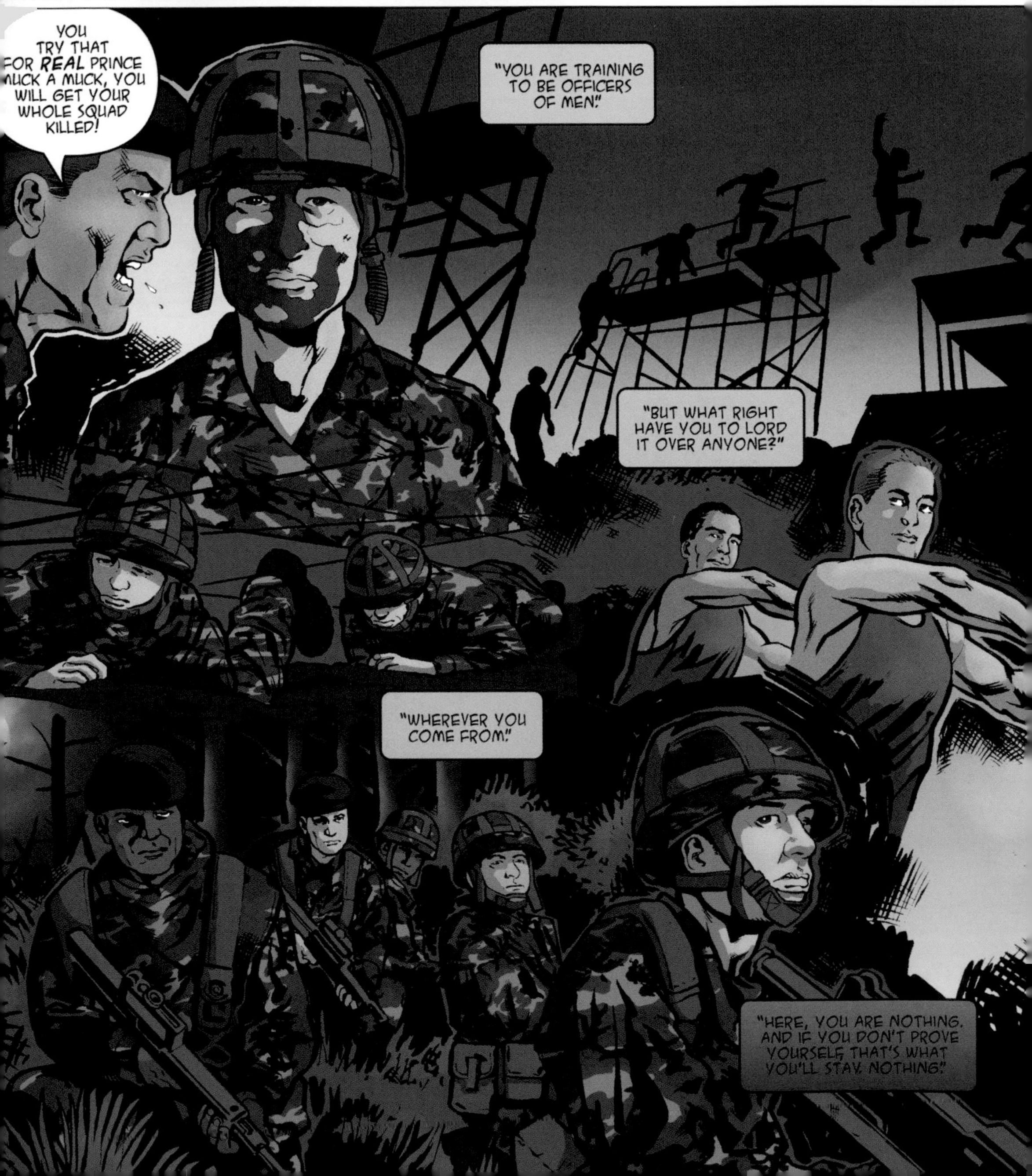
YOU TRY THAT FOR REAL PRINCE MUCK A MUCK, YOU WILL GET YOUR WHOLE SQUAD KILLED!
"YOU ARE TRAINING TO BE OFFICERS OF MEN."
"BUT WHAT RIGHT HAVE YOU TO LORD IT OVER ANYONE?"
"WHEREVER YOU COME FROM."
"HERE, YOU ARE NOTHING. AND IF YOU DON'T PROVE YOURSELF, THAT'S WHAT YOU'LL STAY. NOTHING."

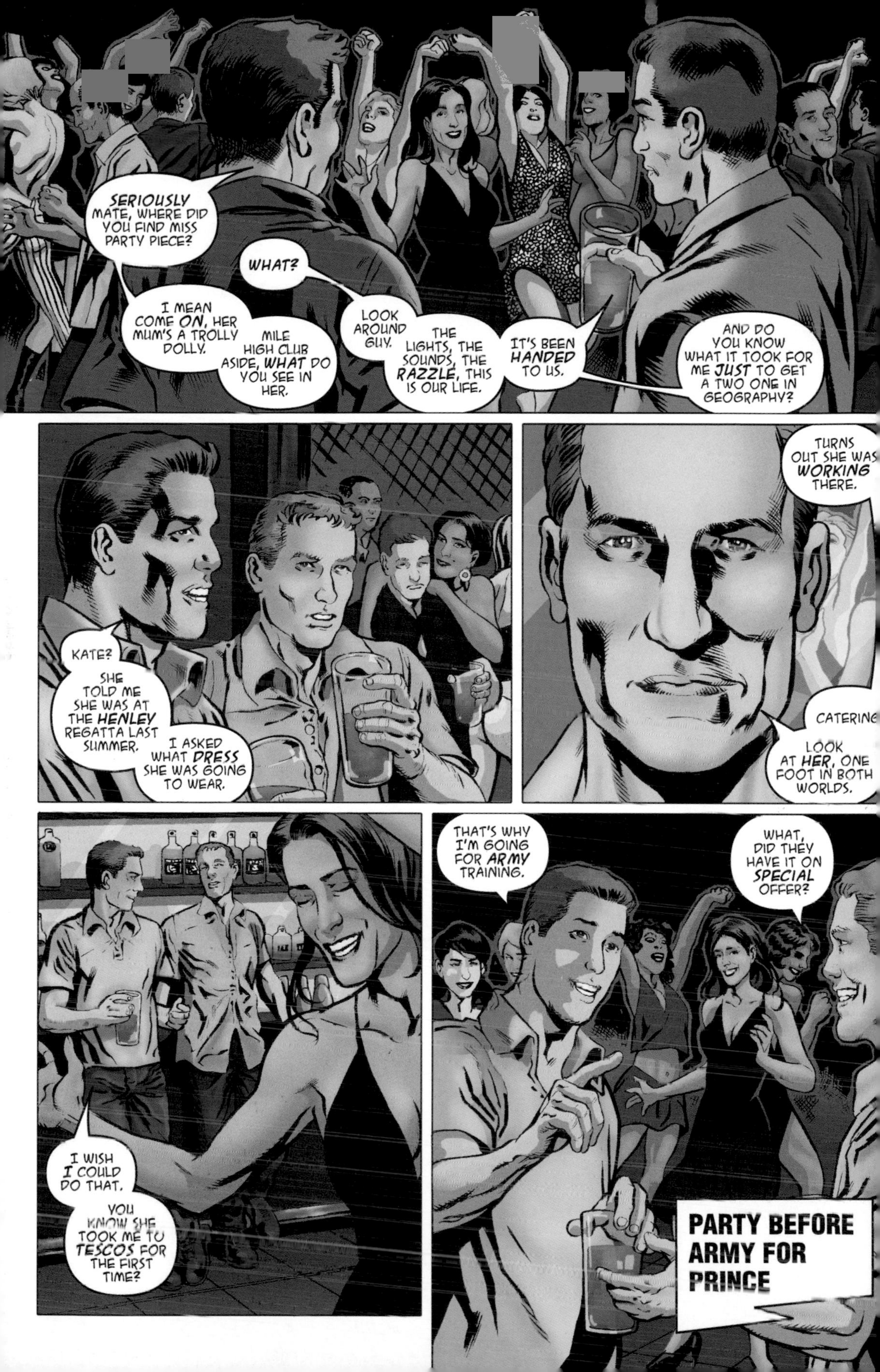
SERIOUSLY MATE, WHERE DID YOU FIND MISS PARTY PIECE?
WHAT?
I MEAN COME ON, HER MUM'S A TROLLY DOLLY.
MILE HIGH CLUB ASIDE, WHAT DO YOU SEE IN HER.
LOOK AROUND GUY.
THE LIGHTS, THE SOUNDS, THE RAZZLE, THIS IS OUR LIFE.
IT'S BEEN HANDED TO US.
AND DO YOU KNOW WHAT IT TOOK FOR ME JUST TO GET A TWO ONE IN GEOGRAPHY?
KATE?
SHE TOLD ME SHE WAS AT THE HENLEY REGATTA LAST SUMMER.
I ASKED WHAT DRESS SHE WAS GOING TO WEAR.
TURNS OUT SHE WAS WORKING THERE.
CATERING
LOOK AT HER, ONE FOOT IN BOTH WORLDS.
I WISH I COULD DO THAT.
YOU KNOW SHE TOOK ME TO TESCOS FOR THE FIRST TIME?
THAT'S WHY I'M GOING FOR ARMY TRAINING.
WHAT, DID THEY HAVE IT ON SPECIAL OFFER?
PARTY BEFORE ARMY FOR PRINCE

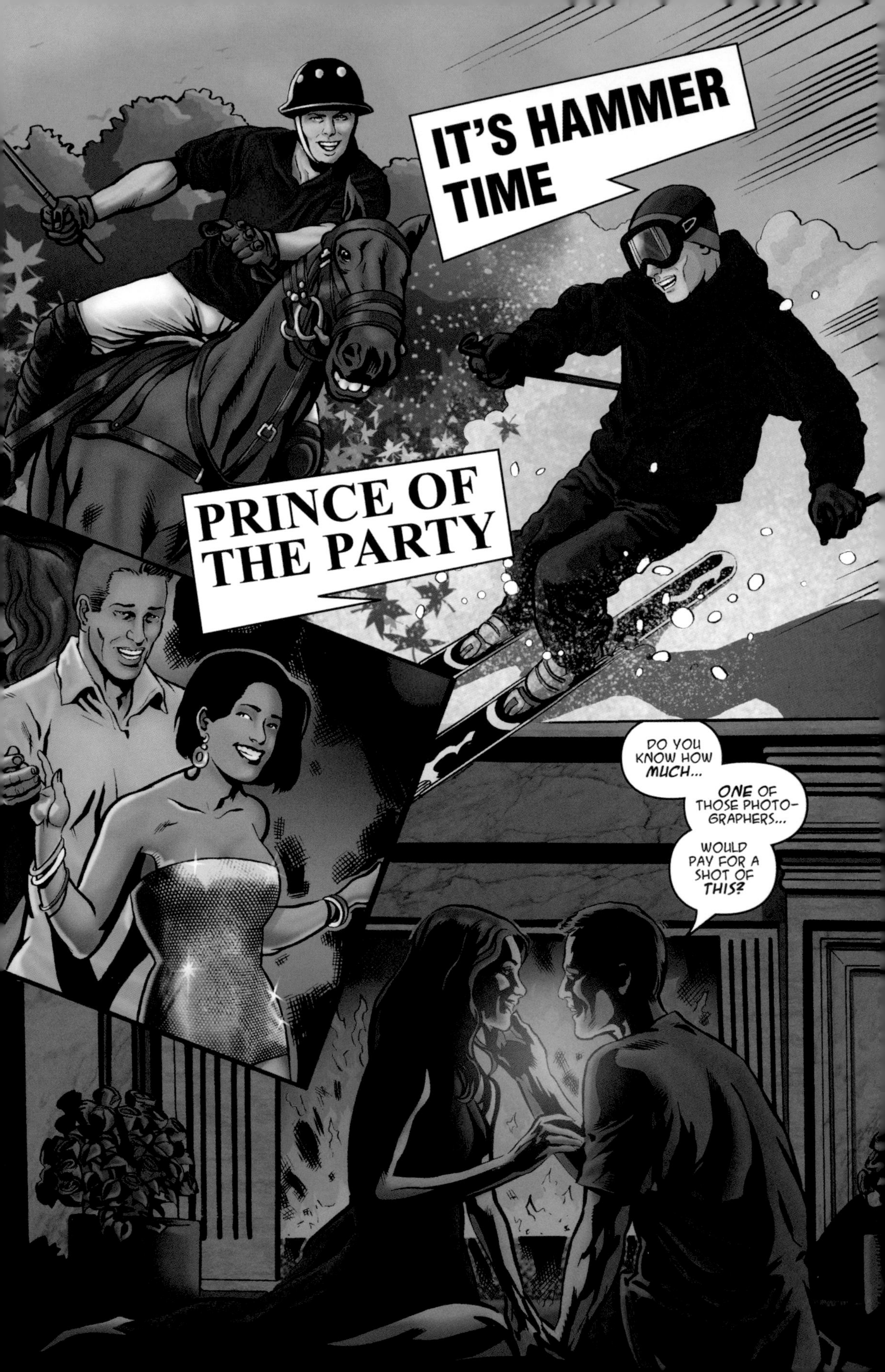
IT'S HAMMER TIME
PRINCE OF THE PARTY
DO YOU KNOW HOW *MUCH*...
ONE OF THOSE PHOTO-GRAPHERS...
WOULD PAY FOR A SHOT OF *THIS?*

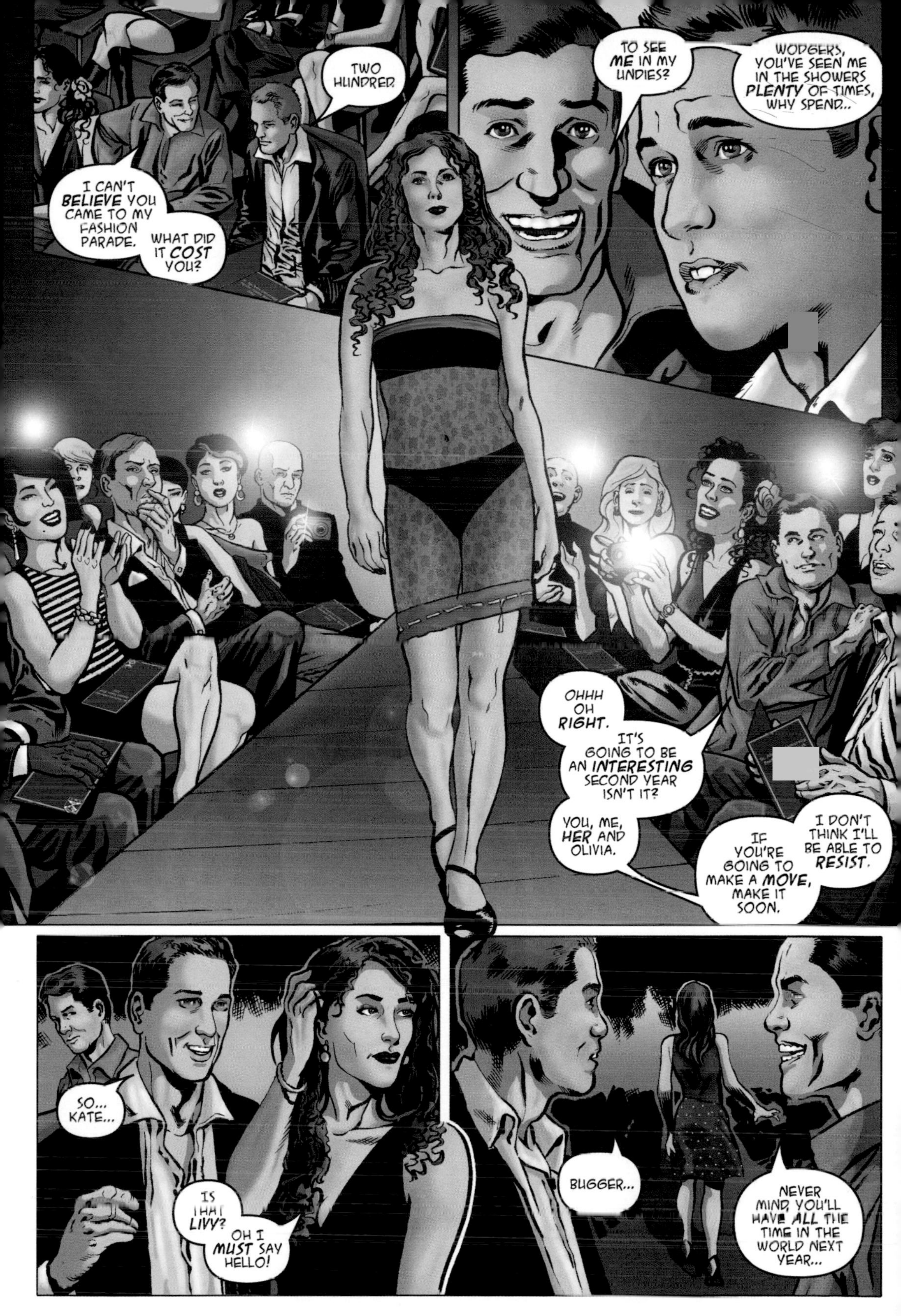
I CAN'T **BELIEVE** YOU CAME TO MY FASHION PARADE.
WHAT DID IT **COST** YOU?
TWO HUNDRED.
TO SEE **ME** IN MY UNDIES?
WODGERS, YOU'VE SEEN ME IN THE SHOWERS **PLENTY** OF TIMES, WHY SPEND...
OHHH OH **RIGHT**.
IT'S GOING TO BE AN **INTERESTING** SECOND YEAR ISN'T IT?
YOU, ME, **HER** AND OLIVIA.
I DON'T THINK I'LL BE ABLE TO **RESIST**.
IF YOU'RE GOING TO MAKE A **MOVE**, MAKE IT SOON.
SO... KATE...
IS THAT **LIVY**?
OH I **MUST** SAY HELLO!
BUGGER...
NEVER MIND, YOU'LL HAVE **ALL** THE TIME IN THE WORLD NEXT YEAR...

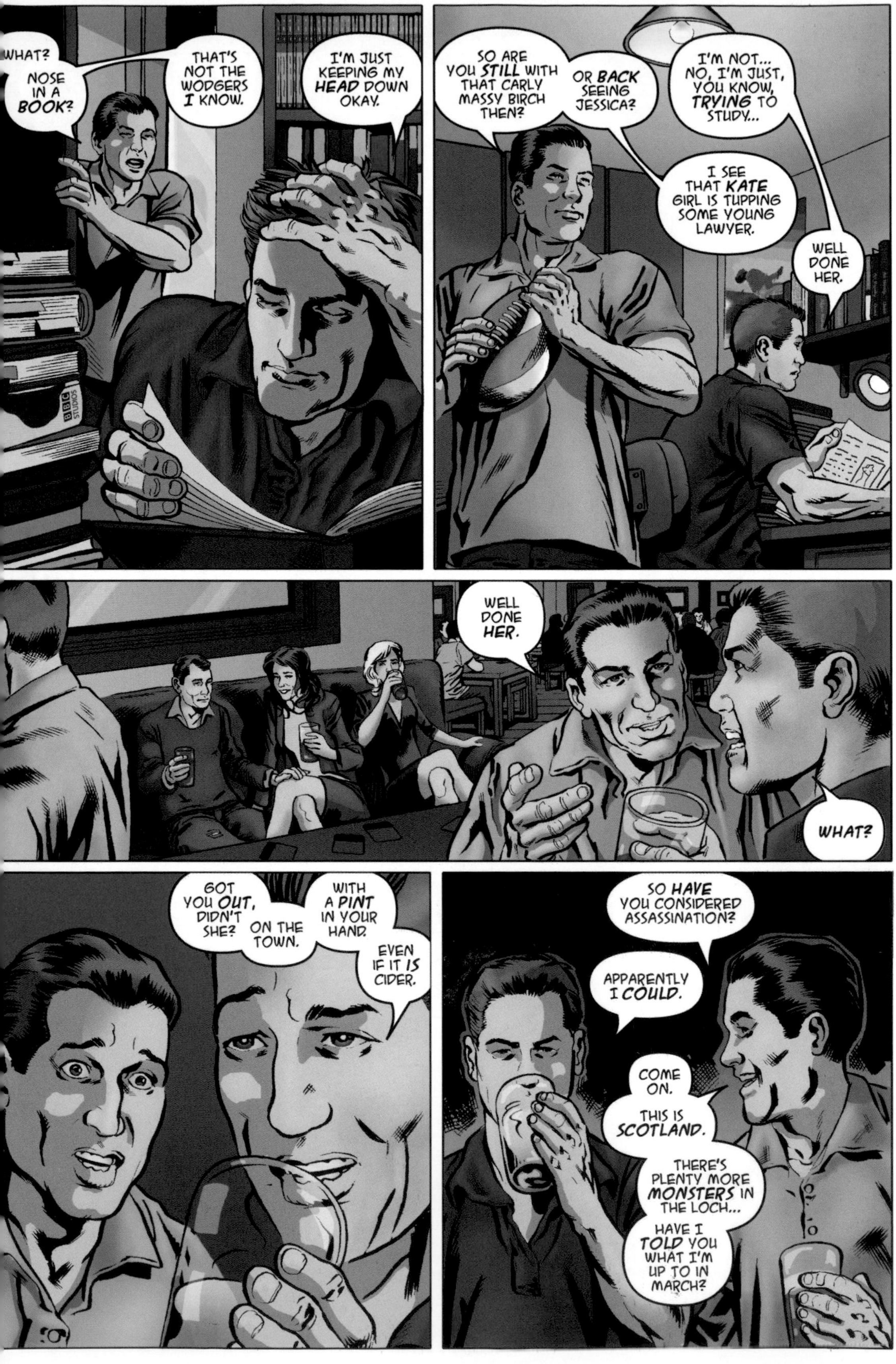

WHAT? NOSE IN A **BOOK**?
THAT'S NOT THE WODGERS **I** KNOW.
I'M JUST KEEPING MY **HEAD** DOWN OKAY.
BBC STUDIOS
SO ARE YOU **STILL** WITH THAT CARLY MASSY BIRCH THEN?
OR **BACK** SEEING JESSICA?
I'M NOT... NO, I'M JUST, YOU KNOW, **TRYING** TO STUDY...
I SEE THAT **KATE** GIRL IS TUPPING SOME YOUNG LAWYER.
WELL DONE HER.
WELL DONE **HER**.
WHAT?
GOT YOU **OUT**, DIDN'T SHE?
ON THE TOWN.
WITH A **PINT** IN YOUR HAND.
EVEN IF IT **IS** CIDER.
SO **HAVE** YOU CONSIDERED ASSASSINATION?
APPARENTLY I **COULD**.
COME ON.
THIS IS **SCOTLAND**.
THERE'S PLENTY MORE **MONSTERS** IN THE LOCH...
HAVE I **TOLD** YOU WHAT I'M UP TO IN MARCH?

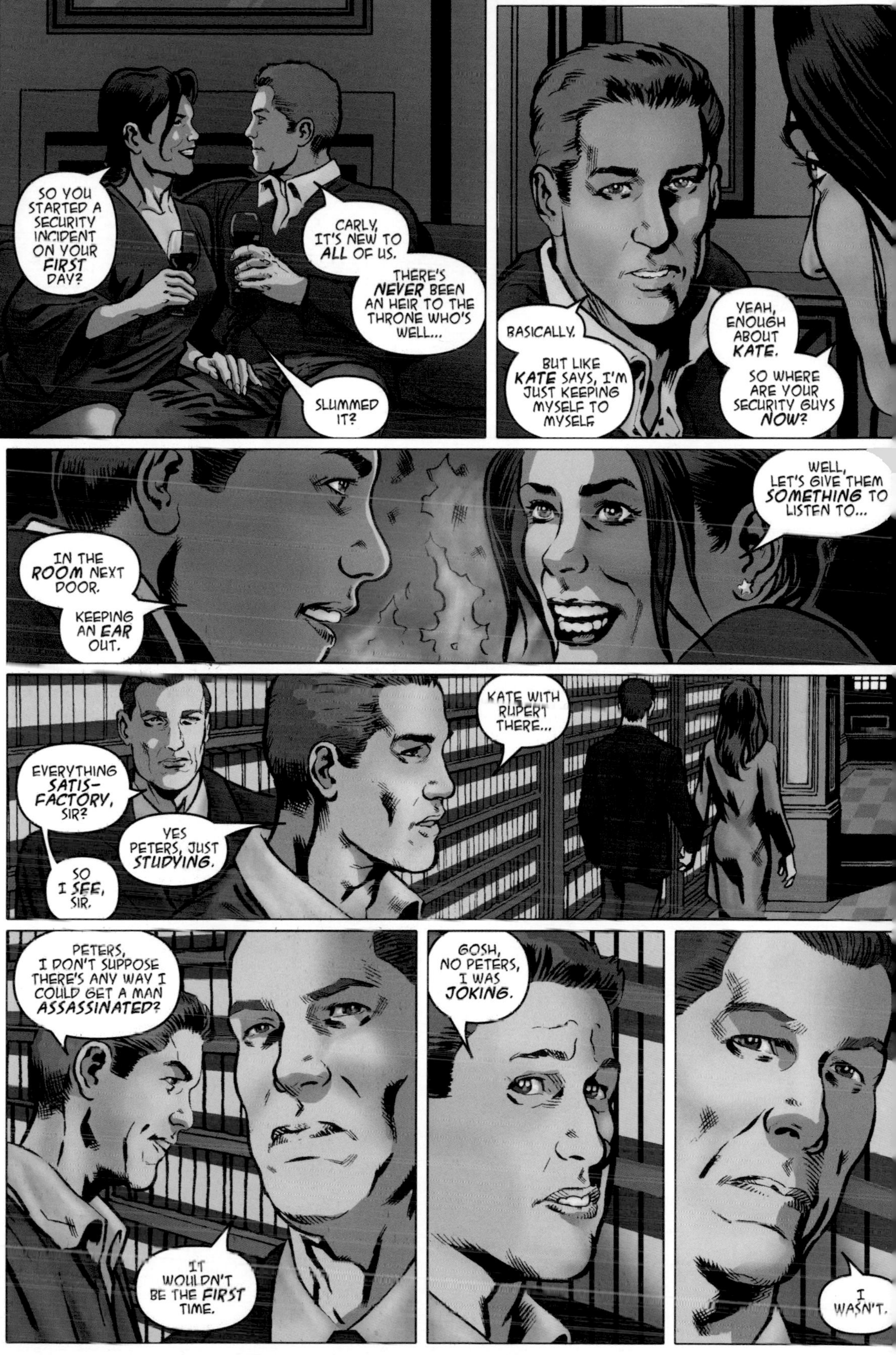
SO YOU STARTED A SECURITY INCIDENT ON YOUR FIRST DAY?
CARLY, IT'S NEW TO ALL OF US.
THERE'S NEVER BEEN AN HEIR TO THE THRONE WHO'S WELL...
SLUMMED IT?
BASICALLY.
BUT LIKE KATE SAYS, I'M JUST KEEPING MYSELF TO MYSELF
YEAH, ENOUGH ABOUT KATE.
SO WHERE ARE YOUR SECURITY GUYS NOW?
IN THE ROOM NEXT DOOR.
KEEPING AN EAR OUT.
WELL, LET'S GIVE THEM SOMETHING TO LISTEN TO...
EVERYTHING SATIS-FACTORY, SIR?
YES PETERS, JUST STUDYING.
SO I SEE, SIR.
KATE WITH RUPERT THERE...
PETERS, I DON'T SUPPOSE THERE'S ANY WAY I COULD GET A MAN ASSASSINATED?
IT WOULDN'T BE THE FIRST TIME.
GOSH, NO PETERS, I WAS JOKING.
I WASN'T.

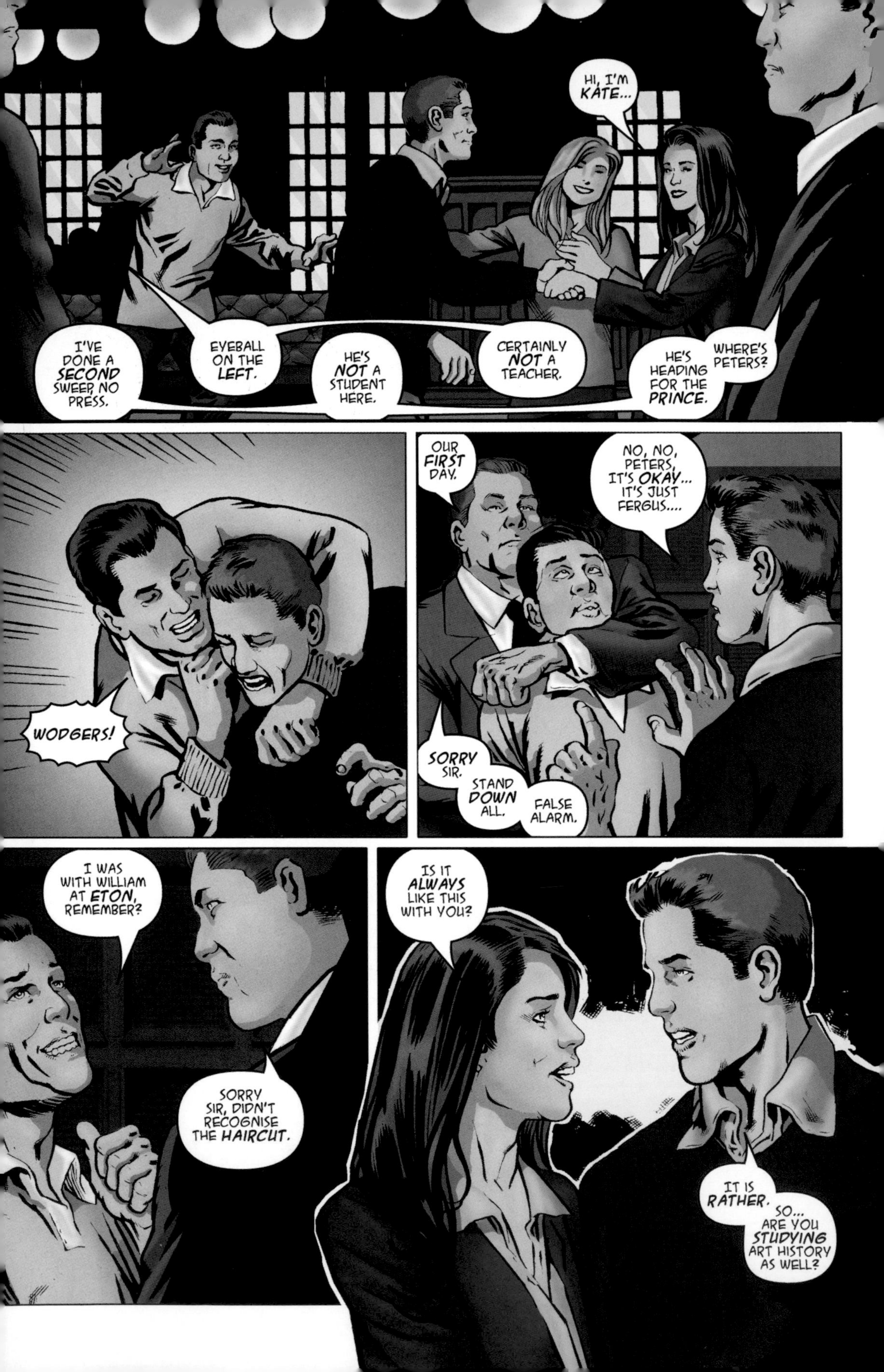
HI, I'M KATE...
I'VE DONE A SECOND SWEEP, NO PRESS.
EYEBALL ON THE LEFT.
HE'S NOT A STUDENT HERE.
CERTAINLY NOT A TEACHER.
WHERE'S PETERS?
HE'S HEADING FOR THE PRINCE.
WODGERS!
OUR FIRST DAY.
NO, NO, PETERS, IT'S OKAY... IT'S JUST FERGUS....
SORRY SIR.
STAND DOWN ALL.
FALSE ALARM.
I WAS WITH WILLIAM AT ETON, REMEMBER?
SORRY SIR, DIDN'T RECOGNISE THE HAIRCUT.
IS IT ALWAYS LIKE THIS WITH YOU?
IT IS RATHER.
SO... ARE YOU STUDYING ART HISTORY AS WELL?

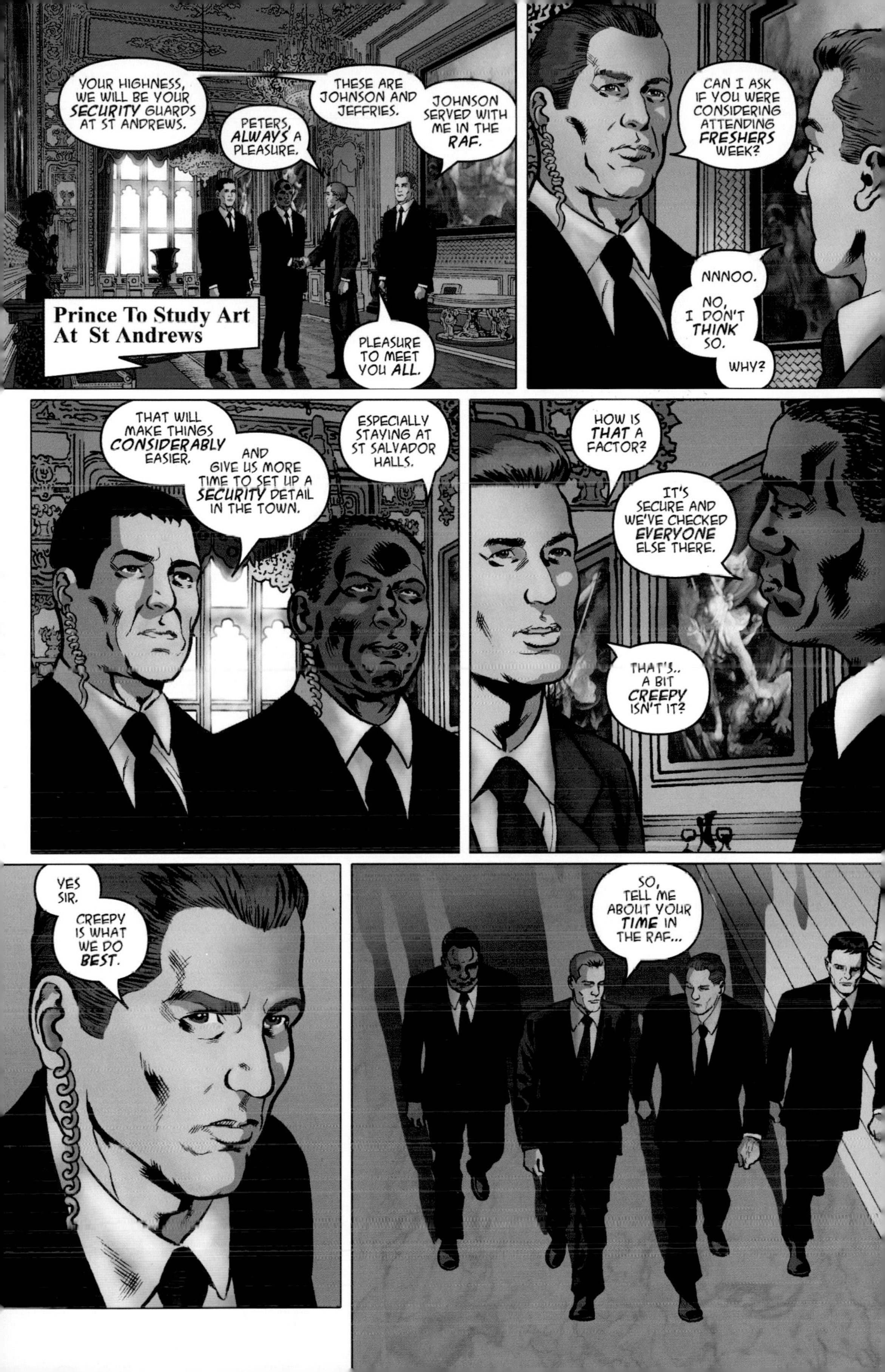

Prince To Study Art At St Andrews
YOUR HIGHNESS, WE WILL BE YOUR SECURITY GUARDS AT ST ANDREWS.
PETERS, ALWAYS A PLEASURE.
THESE ARE JOHNSON AND JEFFRIES.
JOHNSON SERVED WITH ME IN THE RAF.
PLEASURE TO MEET YOU ALL.
CAN I ASK IF YOU WERE CONSIDERING ATTENDING FRESHERS WEEK?
NNNOO.
NO, I DON'T THINK SO.
WHY?
THAT WILL MAKE THINGS CONSIDERABLY EASIER.
AND GIVE US MORE TIME TO SET UP A SECURITY DETAIL IN THE TOWN.
ESPECIALLY STAYING AT ST SALVADOR HALLS.
HOW IS THAT A FACTOR?
IT'S SECURE AND WE'VE CHECKED EVERYONE ELSE THERE.
THAT'S.. A BIT CREEPY ISN'T IT?
YES SIR.
CREEPY IS WHAT WE DO BEST.
SO, TELL ME ABOUT YOUR TIME IN THE RAF...

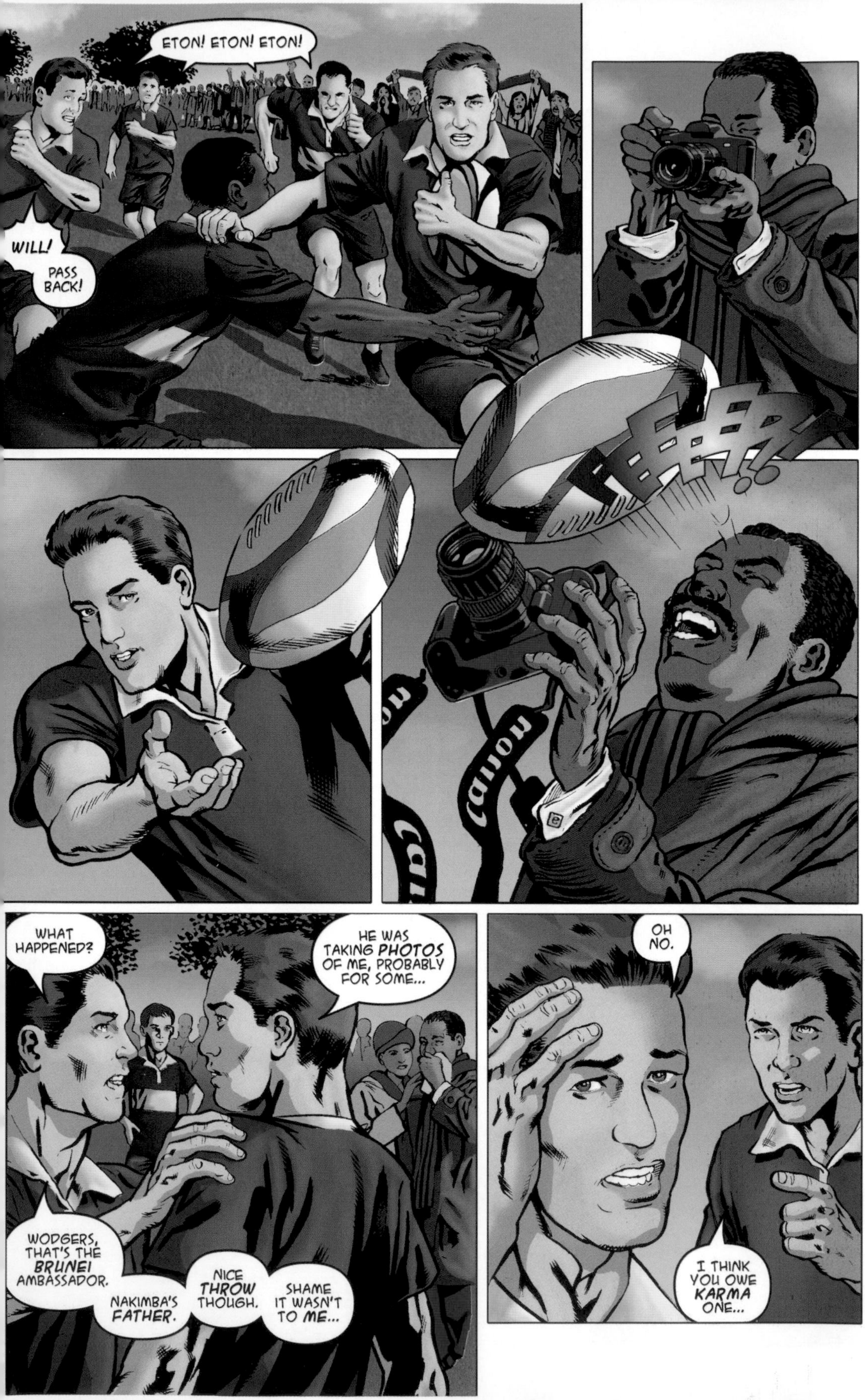
ETON! ETON! ETON!
WILL!
PASS BACK!
WHAT HAPPENED?
HE WAS TAKING **PHOTOS** OF ME, PROBABLY FOR SOME...
WODGERS, THAT'S THE ***BRUNEI*** AMBASSADOR.
NAKIMBA'S ***FATHER***.
NICE ***THROW*** THOUGH.
SHAME IT WASN'T TO ***ME***...
OH NO.
I THINK YOU OWE ***KARMA*** ONE...

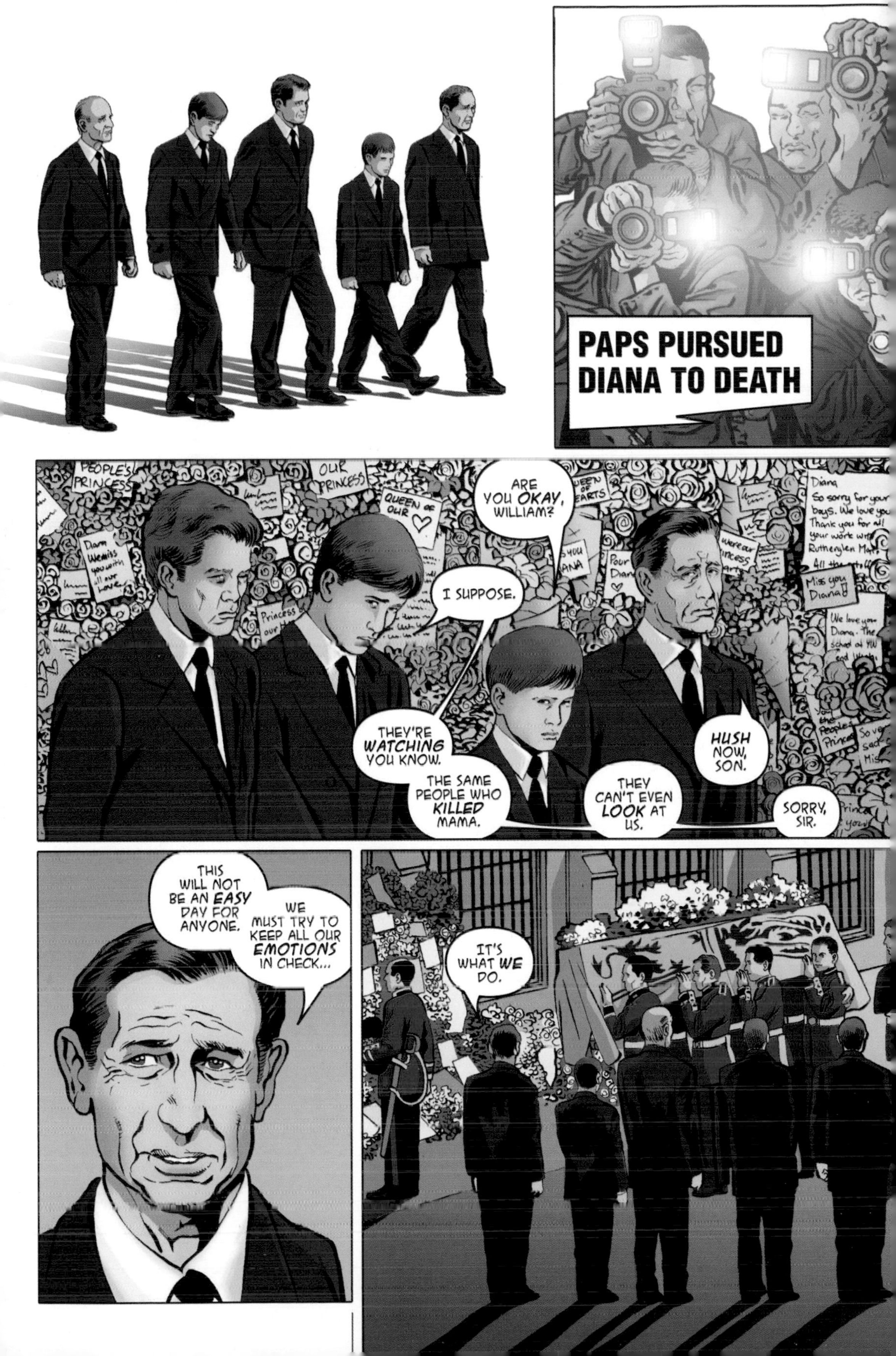
PAPS PURSUED DIANA TO DEATH
PEOPLE'S PRINCESS
OUR PRINCESS
QUEEN OF OUR ♡
QUEEN OF HEARTS
Diana So sorry for your boys. We love you. Thank you for all your work
Miss you Diana!!
ARE YOU OKAY, WILLIAM?
I SUPPOSE.
THEY'RE WATCHING YOU KNOW.
THE SAME PEOPLE WHO KILLED MAMA.
THEY CAN'T EVEN LOOK AT US.
HUSH NOW, SON.
SORRY, SIR.
THIS WILL NOT BE AN EASY DAY FOR ANYONE.
WE MUST TRY TO KEEP ALL OUR EMOTIONS IN CHECK...
IT'S WHAT WE DO.

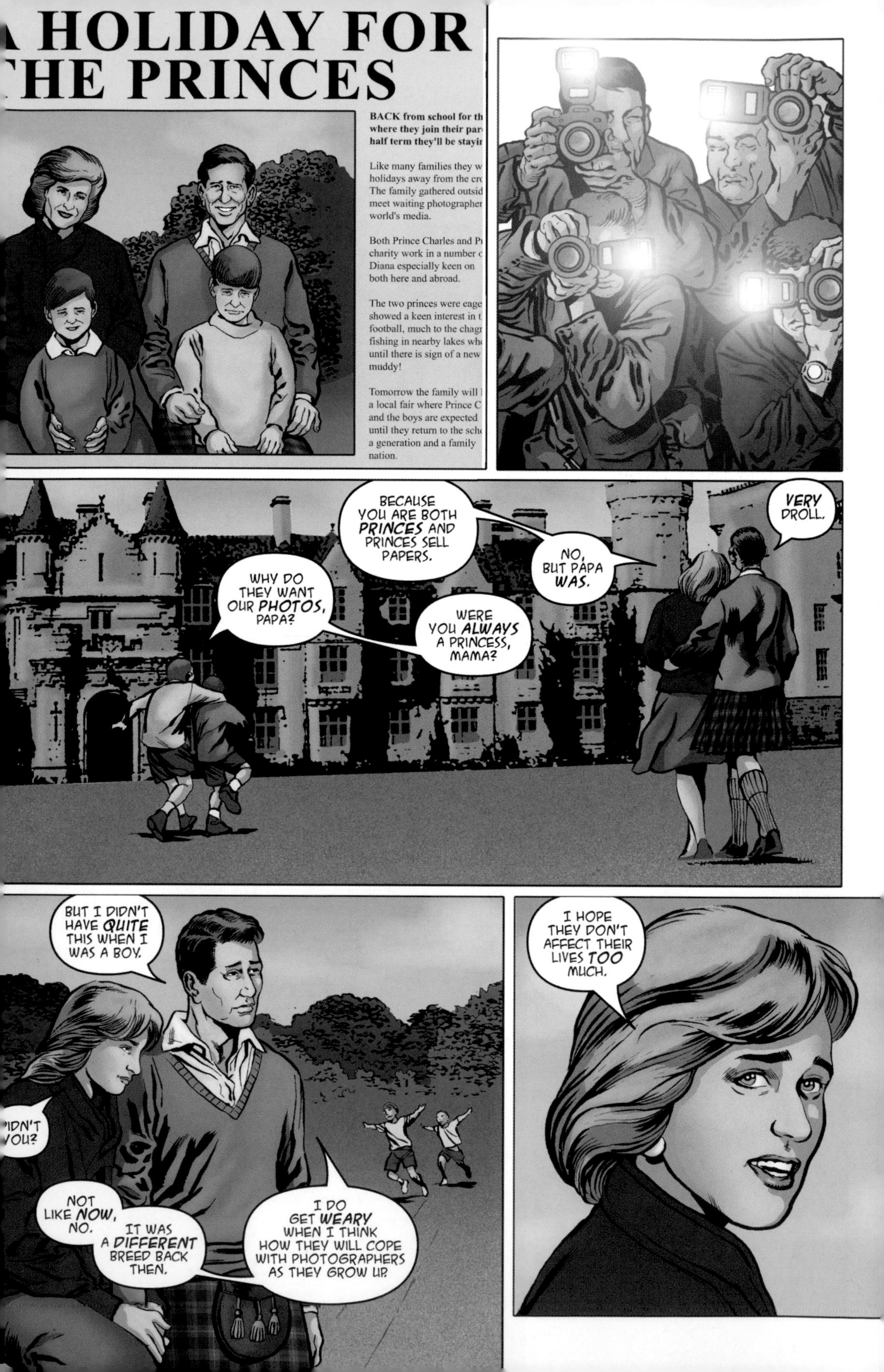
A HOLIDAY FOR
THE PRINCES
BACK from school for th
where they join their par
half term they'll be stayi
Like many families they w
holidays away from the cr
The family gathered outsi
meet waiting photographe
world's media.
Both Prince Charles and P
charity work in a number
Diana especially keen on
both here and abroad.
The two princes were eag
showed a keen interest in
football, much to the chag
fishing in nearby lakes wh
until there is sign of a new
muddy!
Tomorrow the family will
a local fair where Prince C
and the boys are expected
until they return to the sch
a generation and a family
nation.
WHY DO THEY WANT OUR PHOTOS, PAPA?
BECAUSE YOU ARE BOTH PRINCES AND PRINCES SELL PAPERS.
WERE YOU ALWAYS A PRINCESS, MAMA?
NO, BUT PAPA WAS.
VERY DROLL.
BUT I DIDN'T HAVE QUITE THIS WHEN I WAS A BOY.
IDN'T OU?
NOT LIKE NOW, NO.
IT WAS A DIFFERENT BREED BACK THEN.
I DO GET WEARY WHEN I THINK HOW THEY WILL COPE WITH PHOTOGRAPHERS AS THEY GROW UP.
I HOPE THEY DON'T AFFECT THEIR LIVES TOO MUCH.

Windsor of Windsors

A VERY PUBLIC PRINCE

Born William Arthur Philip Louis on June 21, 1982 at St Mary's Hospital, Paddington, west London, he is the elder son of heir-to-the-throne Prince Charles and the late Princess Diana.

After attending Mrs Mynors School, Prince William became a pupil at Wetherby School in London, until 1990 and then Ludgrove School in Berkshire, until 1995. He then attended Eton College. William studied at St Andrews University in Scotland and graduated in Geography in 2005.

Prince William was 15 when Diana, Princess of Wales was killed in a car crash in Paris at the end of August 1997. William and his younger brother Prince Harry walked behind their mother's cortege at her funeral procession in London.

After a gap year in which he visited Chile, Belize, worked on British dairy farms and visited countries in Africa, Prince William chose to study at St Andrews University in Fife, Scotland. He graduated with a 2:1 in Geography in 2005.

William joined the Royal Military Academy Sandhurst as an Officer Cadet and was commissioned as an army officer in front of the Queen at Sandhurst in December 2006 and joined the Household Cavalry (Blues and Royals) as a Second Lieutenant.

On St George's Day (23rd April 2008) The Queen appointed Prince William to be a Royal Knight Companion of the Most Noble Order of the Garter. He was installed at The Annual Garter ceremony held at Windsor Castle.

William graduated as a search and rescue Pilot with the Royal Air Force in September 2010, based at Anglesey, Wales.

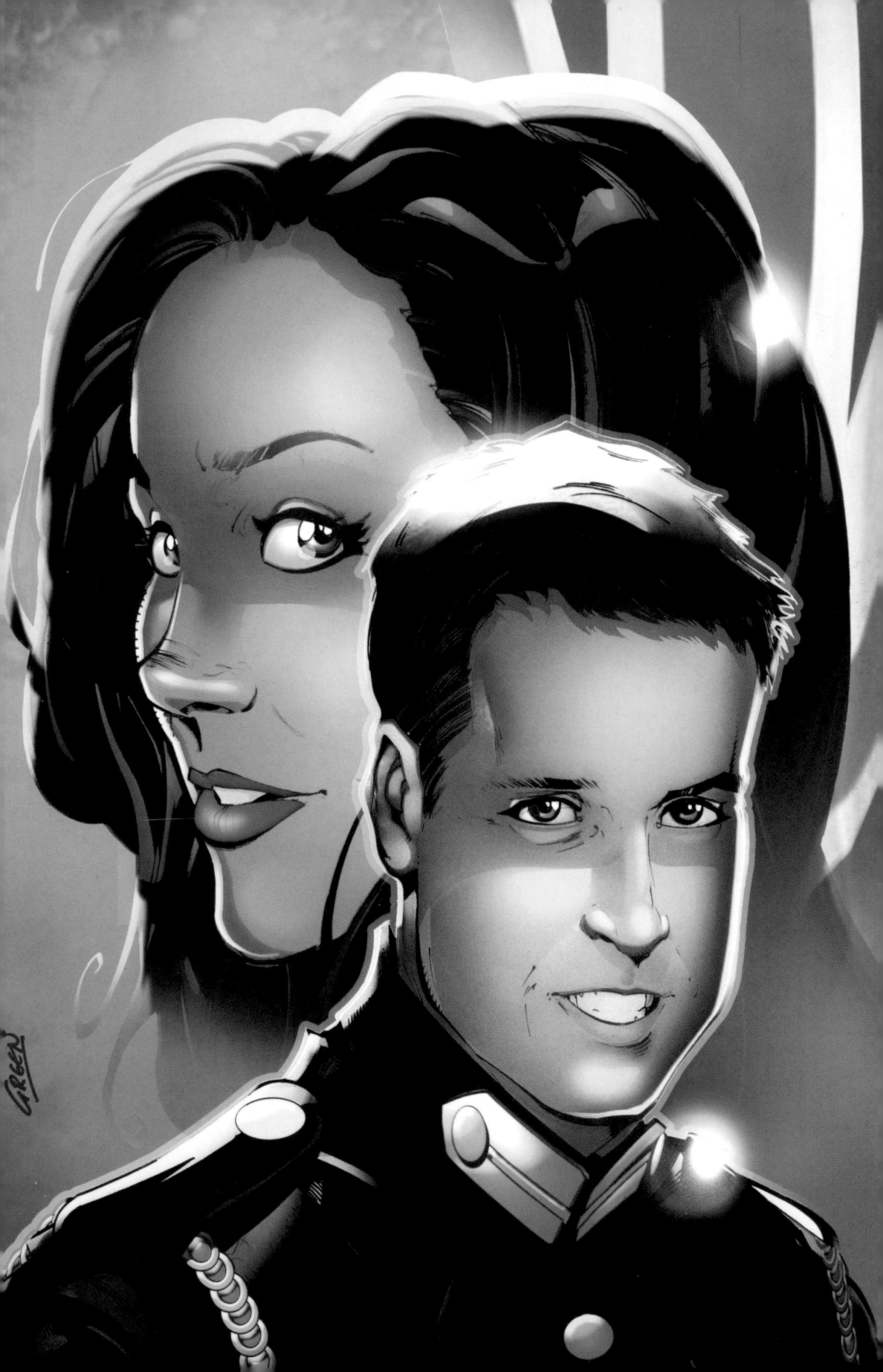
GREEN

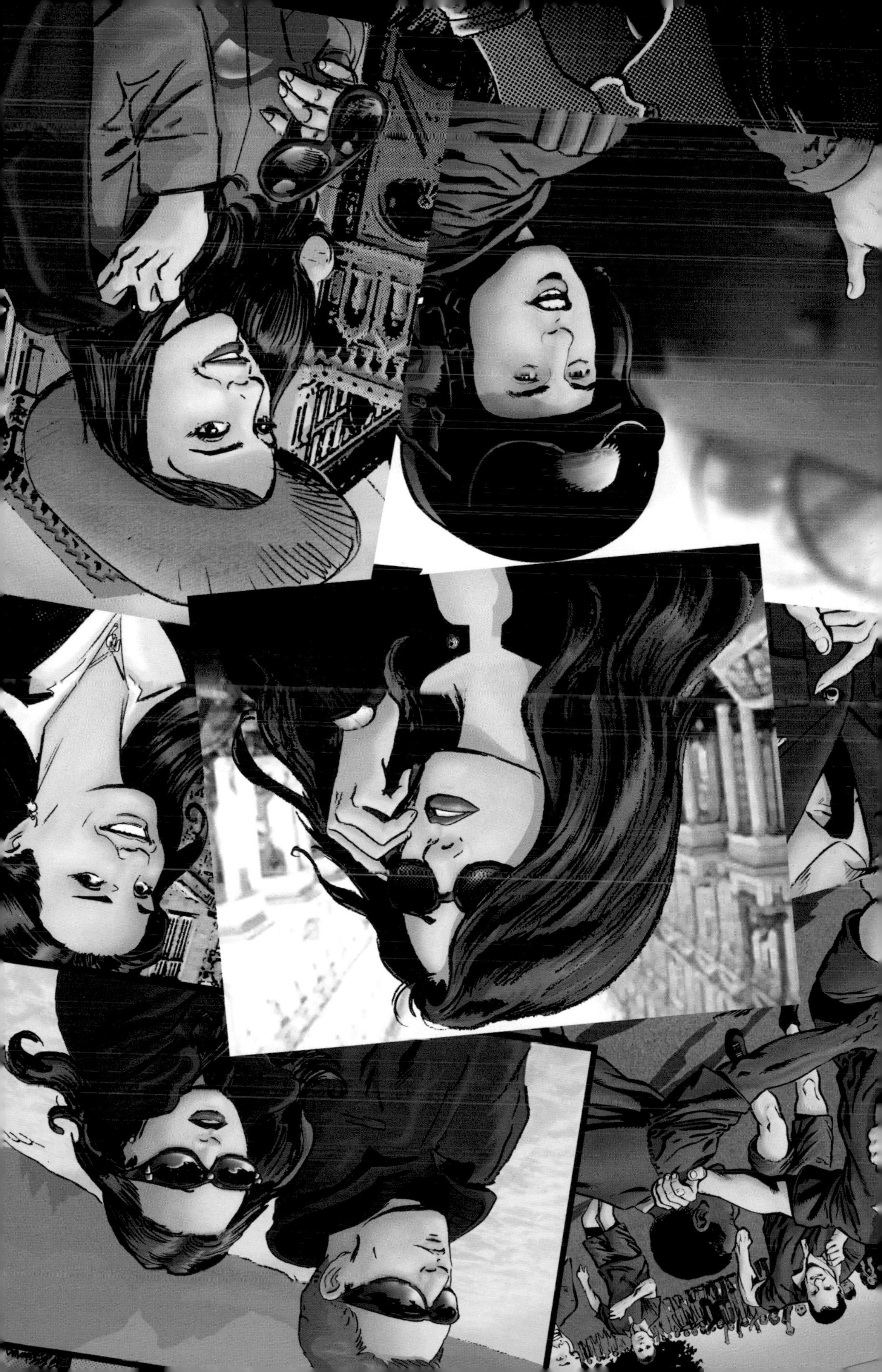

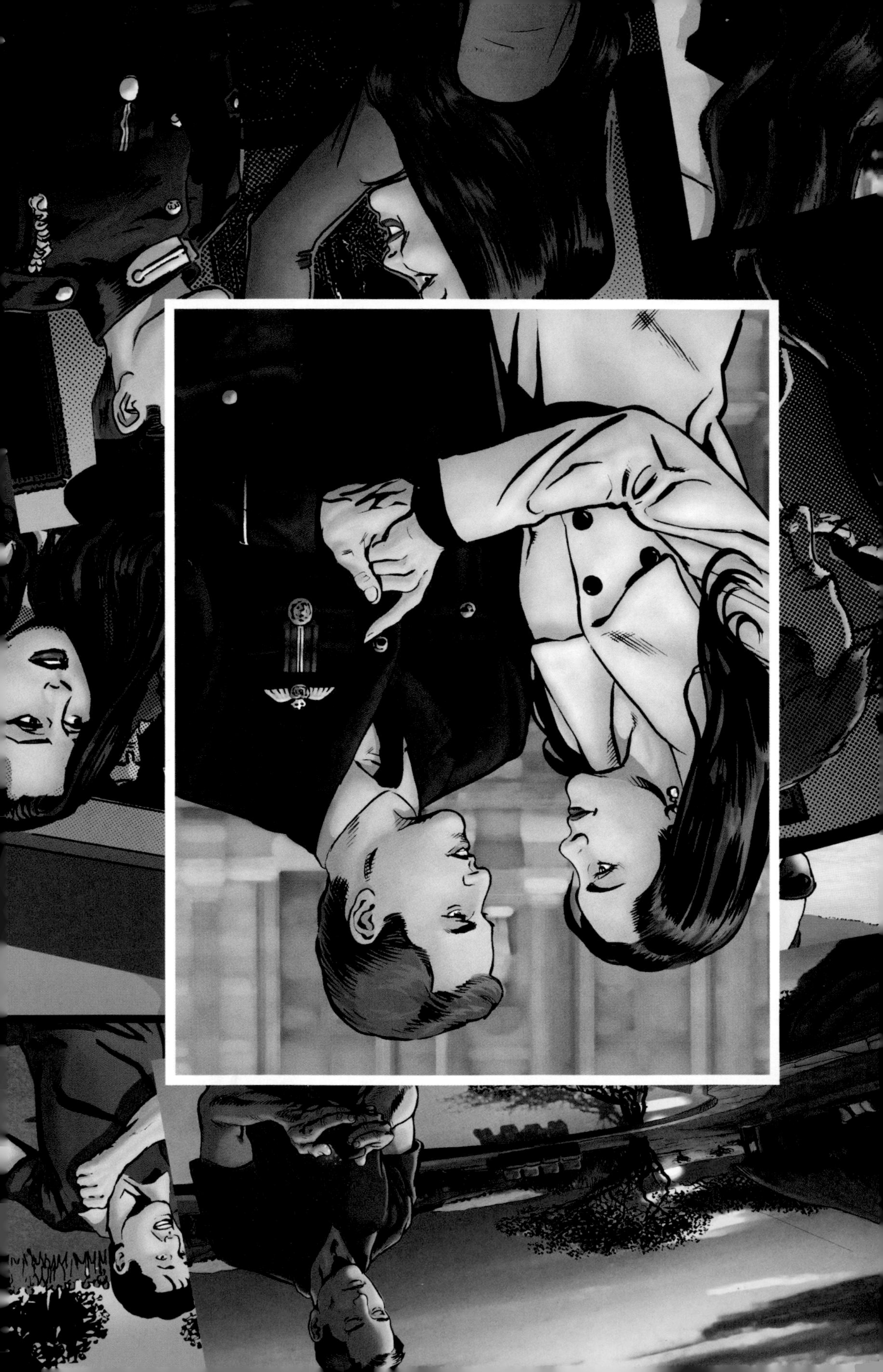

A VERY PUBLIC
PRINCE

Written by: **Rich Johnston**

Art by: **Gary Erskine**

Colours by: **Owen Jollands of Hayena Studios**

Letters by: **Ian Sharman**

Pin ups: **Paul Green**

THIS IS A FLIP BOOK:
If you'd like to start reading with Kate's story,
please flip the book over and begin reading
from the other end!

For Markosia Enterprises Ltd

Harry Markos
Publisher & Managing partner

Huw-J
Art Director

Ian Sharman ♦ GM Jordan ♦ Andy Briggs
Group Editors

ISBN:978-1905692-45-3

AAM/MARKOSIA

A VERY PUBLIC LOVE STORY

SHARMAN

◆

JOLLANDS

◆

ERSKINE

◆

COLLINS

◆

JOHNSTON

Kate & William